ASPECTS OF
EURIPIDEAN TRAGEDY

ASPECTS OF
EURIPIDEAN TRAGEDY

BY

L. H. G. GREENWOOD

Fellow of Emmanuel College
Cambridge

CAMBRIDGE
AT THE UNIVERSITY PRESS
1953

CAMBRIDGE
UNIVERSITY PRESS

University Printing House, Cambridge CB2 8BS, United Kingdom

Cambridge University Press is part of the University of Cambridge.

It furthers the University's mission by disseminating knowledge in the pursuit of education, learning and research at the highest international levels of excellence.

www.cambridge.org
Information on this title: www.cambridge.org/9781107559806

© Cambridge University Press 1953

First published 1953
First paperback edition 2015

A catalogue record for this publication is available from the British Library

ISBN 978-1-107-55980-6 Paperback

CONTENTS

PREFACE

Some apology is perhaps due to the reader for this book's lack of unity. The first three of its five chapters, indeed, have a single theme. They state an old problem, and propound and defend a new solution of it. But the fourth and fifth chapters have different subjects; and the fifth is concerned with an aspect of Greek tragedy generally, not with Euripides only. The bearing of these chapters on the subject of the first three, though real, is slight and indirect; and such interest and importance as they possess must lie in themselves.

I owe much to the helpful criticism of several friends. My debt is especially great to Professor Kitto: all the greater because many of my arguments and conclusions do not, I think, command his assent.

The English verse renderings in the fourth chapter are my own, based on Professor Murray's Oxford text, from which I have quoted such passages as my argument needed.

L. H. G. G.

CAMBRIDGE
January 1952

CHAPTER I

THE FANTASY THEORY: A NEW SOLUTION OF AN OLD PROBLEM

THE main purpose of this small book is to put forward
and defend a new solution of one of the major difficulties
that confront the student of Euripides: namely, that
whereas the poet's representation of the nature and
actions of the gods, in many of his plays if not in all,
conflicts sharply with what appear to be his own religious
beliefs, nevertheless these gods and their activities are
presented as an integral and irremovable element of the
whole. None of the ways in which this difficulty has
hitherto been dealt with can be held fully satisfactory.
The way here followed is to suppose, first, that the plots
of the plays, or of most of them, are *fantasies*: that is, series
of events which Euripides neither himself thought, nor
wished the enlightened among his audience and his
readers to think, such as actually occurred or could have
occurred. And secondly, that this is all: that there is no
second version of the plot, no 'real story', underlying
what is on the surface.

The distinctive feature of this solution is the conjunction of these two propositions. Neither of them, taken
by itself, is wholly novel. The first, or something like it,
forms part of the line of interpretation adopted by Verrall
and his followers, whom I may describe as 'rationalists'.
It would also be maintained by those whom I may call
'symbolists', who interpret the Olympian deities as
symbols, for Euripides, of forces of nature. But rationa-

lists and symbolists agree in supposing further that Euripides has a second and 'real' story to put before us. It is not the story that first meets our eyes; it is under the surface, and must be looked for; but it is there. My second proposition is part of what may be called, conveniently if somewhat vaguely and recklessly, the ordinary view: the view which tends to ignore, or to brush aside, the facts and arguments that constitute the difficulty in question; to deny the need of a second meaning because the first and obvious meaning will do well enough, or, if not well enough, as well as we have any good reason to require and expect of Euripides. In this view, what first meets our eyes is the real story, and Euripides neither has any other to suggest to us, nor wishes to imply that there is anything amiss with the one he offers us. The rationalist and symbolist views are right, I think, in holding that he does not believe in the literal truth of the story he seems to present. The ordinary view is right in holding that he presents no other story. All three views are mistaken in holding that he does nevertheless present a story which he thinks, and therefore means others to think, either actually or at least possibly true.

This preliminary statement of my theory may at once raise two distinct objections. The first is that such plays would have no clear purpose or meaning. How, it may be asked, could Euripides, or any other poet, think it worth while to produce a series of stories that were not only fictions but impossible fictions? What purpose, what meaning could such productions have for any part of his audience? A possible fiction might indeed serve some purpose and have some meaning; we know from Aristotle that Agathon, anticipating the novel, tried the experiment. But an impossible fiction? In the second place, suppose some plausible purpose and meaning could be suggested even for this, yet on a stage where for generations the 'sacred history', and sometimes the events of recent times, had been shown as a record of fact, how could a thing so utterly different be tolerated, or even understood? Would not the offence against religious propriety, against artistic tradition, against mere 'good form', be resented, promptly, vigorously and universally, by the Athenian people? Let the suggested difficulty be never so serious, and the proposed solution of it never so adequate, must not the solution raise a difficulty more serious than that which it is designed to remove?

No single statement, no one simple argument, can meet these objections fully. It will be convenient to begin by attempting to meet the second. In the first place, we may observe that Euripides' point of view (if it is what I suppose) is not, as a rule, obtruded. It is seldom emphasized in any way; very seldom expressed plainly, in so many words; never, owing to the nature of tragic drama, so expressed as to make it immediately and obviously certain that the poet himself is speaking, using his personages as mouthpieces of his own opinions, and not making them speak in character. His method is that of irony and innuendo: he 'implies things'. On the surface, all, or nearly all, is straightforward, conventional, orthodox. The story presented is, in its main outlines and often in its details, that of received tradition. The details were not fixed by tradition; there was always room for the poet to choose among variants already current, or to invent new variants of his own; when Euripides did so, he was only doing what others were doing and had always done, and his plots were in any case, to say the least of it, not less orthodox than those of

3

others. Many of those who saw and read his plays would find nothing amiss. To many, the mere visible appearance of the gods in person, behaving in a way wholly consonant with tradition, would dispel any suspicions of his orthodoxy that might have been raised by their hearing some unusual opinion uttered by one of his characters: even as today Christian congregations are more apt to suspect and resent innovations in visible ritual than doctrinal novelties merely heard from the pulpit. Other Athenians, more intelligent or better informed, and therefore inclined to suspect, or even able to detect, the poet's concealed unbelief, would yet tolerate what they saw and heard, provided external decency were observed: not perhaps quite liking it all, but finding no occasion for active resentment in his treatment of matters about which, after all, the facts were admittedly hard to ascertain. Others, again, and these perhaps not a small minority, would not merely tolerate but approve and enjoy: enjoy the irony, and approve the poet's serious purpose—of which more later. So long, therefore, as impossible fiction was presented as if it were actual fact, the poet might safely go some way towards revealing his own conviction that it was not actual or even possible fact. The revelation has certainly escaped the majority of his readers in these days: it is the less likely to have been offensively obvious to his contemporaries.

In the second place, though the theory certainly implies that Euripides was, in this matter, breaking with tradition, yet the break, obvious or not, generally detected or not, was perhaps less violent than the objection implies that it was. We are not entitled to assume, as a matter of course, that it would be considered essential, or even highly important, that the events represented on

4

the ancient tragic stage should be clearly possible events. From the general character of the surviving tragedies of Aeschylus and Sophocles we may indeed infer that the clearly impossible was avoided as a rule. But was the avoidance of it a prime necessity? Would the introduction of it be sure to give offence? The *Prometheus* and the *Eumenides* at least suggest the contrary. So does the fact that the outward form of all Greek tragedy was intensely conventional, as far removed as the opera of the eighteenth and early nineteenth centuries from any realistic reproduction of the speech and behaviour of actual life.[1] For however vividly actual life was conveyed to the spectator, however distinctly it was perceived under its cloak of conventional form, yet the extreme conventionality of the form must have been capable of disguising, to some extent, any failure of the substance to conform with what was held actually probable or even possible. In our own time, any such discrepancy would escape notice far more easily in a stylized opera than in a realistic play. Even, therefore, if Euripides' plots had been more obviously impossible than they were, and his view of them as such more sharply emphasized than it was, we cannot be sure that the Athenians would have resented his not giving them something which in any case they had not always been given by other tragic poets, and which they had never, consciously at least, expected any tragic poet to give them. To them, the novelty of his method would probably seem to lie not so much in the impossibility itself as in his deliberately drawing their attention to it; and owing to the delicate subtlety with which he commonly did this, not everyone would see that he was doing it, and not everyone who saw it would resent it.

[1] My fifth chapter discusses this subject at length.

The two arguments already put forward do not depend, for any force they may have as answers to the objections they are meant to answer, on the precise nature of the impossibility that my theory attributes to Euripides' plots. But if we now ask in what that impossibility consists, the objections may appear still less formidable; and in particular, we may begin to see an answer to the first of them, which was that my theory robs the plays of any clear purpose or satisfactory meaning. It is now time to explain more fully the sense in which I use the word 'fantasy' to describe Euripides' plays, or some of them; and perhaps not only to explain, but to apologize for using the word as I do. It commonly suggests, for one thing, the notion of incoherence; and I am so far from thinking the plays incoherent, in any way, that it is my express purpose to offer a fresh and satisfactory reason for thinking them far more coherent than what I have called the ordinary view seems content to suppose. The word may further suggest that I regard the plots as impossible in all their parts alike, and from every point of view. Now I do maintain that the several plots are impossible *as wholes*. But this is not the same thing as maintaining that all the parts of these wholes, all the particular events, are impossible. Many of them, indeed most of them, are not only possible but probable; and this in two senses. They are probable unconditionally, as obeying the laws of nature and in particular the laws of human nature; and they are probable conditionally, as following naturally from the events that precede them. It is in fact only the divine personages whose words and deeds are, as Euripides thinks and would have others think, unconditionally impossible. The impossibility of each plot as a whole is due to the fact that the activities of the divine personages

6

form an integral and irremovable part of the whole: due to this fact, and to this fact only.

'The stories I put before you', Euripides in effect says to his audience and his readers, 'cannot be true; for they imply that the gods are such beings, and do such actions, as no right-minded and sensible man can think possible. None the less, tradition represents the gods as such beings, and as acting thus; and if you can and will believe tradition in this matter, there is no reason why you should find my plots impossible or even improbable. But even if you cannot or will not believe tradition, there is a quite definite element of possibility and even probability in these plots. I am showing you what, *if* tradition were trustworthy, *if* the gods were like that, might have happened or even must have happened. For my human personages, I will venture to claim, are more real, they behave more naturally, than those of other tragic poets. I show you human beings feeling, speaking and acting in a manner that accords with the observed facts of human nature and human conduct. Sophocles meant this, though he did not mean it as praise of me, when he said that I depict men as they are. *If*, therefore, the tales of the gods and their dealings with men were true, men *would* have behaved just as I show them behaving. I may therefore claim that a part of my stories, and a very important part, is true, in spite of the fact that—the strength of a chain being the strength of its weakest link—the stories as a whole are, and must be, impossible fictions.'

If, in putting such words into Euripides' mouth, I represent his aims and attitude correctly—as I shall presently try to show that I do—this much at least becomes clearer, that my theory need not be rejected out of hand on the ground that his audience and readers would not have tolerated so great a departure from the customs of the tragic stage as the theory implies. I have already argued that possibility, in a plot, is a quality that was neither consciously demanded of tragic poets nor invariably supplied by them; I now urge that the plots of Euripides nevertheless have this quality, from at least one important point of view, in a high degree. It is because they have it, and in a high degree, that Euripides is 'the most tragic of the poets', that he can excite in us the pity and terror which no mere phantasmagoria, no tale of events wholly unwarranted by the known facts of life, could possibly arouse. The toleration of his plays, in spite of their being what I suppose, needs explanation only so far as concerns those of his audience, perhaps not a very large proportion of the whole, who both detected his attitude towards traditional religion and also disapproved of it; and if he gave even these persons so much else to interest and satisfy them, so much that not only was what they had always desired and got, but was, or might well seem, better than anything yet given them, then even these persons would at least tolerate his work, if they could not heartily approve it. And note that it is only toleration, not hearty approval, with which my theory has to be shown compatible. It is well known that Euripides' plays were less successful, and less widely popular, in his lifetime than they became after his death. Whatever the cause or causes of this, the real problem is not why in his lifetime they were liked so much, but why they were not liked still more; and my theory is so far from making *this* problem more insoluble that it does at least as much, I think, as any other theory can do to solve it.

But, it may be asked, is not the first objection more than ever in need of answer? Does not my recognition

of Euripides' earnest concern with the realities of life at
once make my conception of his plays as impossible
fictions much less plausible? Is not a story in which
the actions and fortunes of human beings are shown
as the effects of causes that do not and cannot exist
a most unsatisfactory story? Why did not Euripides
do in all his plays what he has done in some of them
—show human fortunes as the effects of causes that
do exist and are recognized by all intelligent men?
Is it not more probable that he did do this in all
his plays alike, and that his plots do after all represent,
not partially but wholly, events that could have
occurred?

Such arguments would be formidable but for one
consideration. If we examine the plots of those plays in
which the direct intervention of the gods is, or appears
to be, an integral part of the story, we shall find nearly
always that the feelings and actions and fate of the
human persons, though shown as the effects of supernatural causes, are in their essence such as are commonly
the effects of natural causes. It is quite easy to imagine
versions of the *Ion*, the *Heracles*, the *Hippolytus*, the
Bacchae, in which, with a slight alteration of the plot, all
that is essential in the human story could be preserved,
in spite of the complete elimination of supernatural
agencies. Ion's father might have been a mortal.
Heracles' madness might have been the 'natural'
collapse of a great but unstable mind. Phaedra's passion
for Hippolytus might have been 'due to natural causes',
a normal case of falling in love. The fate of Pentheus
might have been what the fate of Orpheus was, the
hideous but natural outcome of religious fanaticism.
Apollo, Hera, Aphrodite, Dionysus are not indispensable
for stories that would, in all respects that matter for

9

them as pictures of human life, have been the same as the stories we have actually presented to us.

It is this consideration that lies at the bottom of the 'rationalist' and 'symbolist' solutions of our problem. These solutions will in due course be examined in detail; but it may be said at once that both of them are *prima facie* reasonable. Neither of them, as I hope to show, will stand close examination; and yet both of them come near the truth. They are alike wrong in seeking to interpret the story Euripides gives us as a presentation of what could happen. But they are alike right in making us feel that the story he gives us is so similar to another story, a story he does not give us, that the human significance of the story he does give us would hardly have been affected if he had actually given us the other. *Macbeth* and *Hamlet* may suggest useful parallels. Whatever Shakespeare and his contemporaries believed about witches and ghosts, it is certain that modern readers who believe in neither do not look on these dramas as meaningless and uninteresting, as having no real bearing on human life, merely because the tragic events are shown as directly caused, in part at least, by agencies whose existence we reject. If we can, and do, 'suspend' our disbelief in such agencies, it is because we feel instinctively that agencies in which we do believe could produce the same effects, and might easily have been substituted by Shakespeare for those he has chosen to give us. It is not hard to suppose that Euripides' contemporaries were capable of similar instinctive feelings. We can probably detect them in ourselves when we read his plays. Our interest in Phaedra and Hippolytus is of the same kind, and as real and intense, as our interest in Medea and Jason, though the direct activity of a deity is essential in the story of the *Hippolytus* as we have it, and plays almost no part in the story of the *Medea*. While, then, we may and must admit, and indeed insist, that Euripides' main purpose was to show us what men are and do and suffer, we are not for that reason bound to admit that this main purpose must be wrecked, or even hampered, by being combined with a subsidiary purpose that nevertheless converts the plot from a representation of fact into a representation of fiction.

Two of the extant plays—I think two only—may seem to contravene the principle stated in the last paragraph. These are the *Alcestis* and the *Helena*. In each of these the supernatural element in the plot is of such a kind, and is so related to the main human interest of the play, that it is hard to imagine natural causation substituted for supernatural without drastic alteration of the human story. Natural causation is clearly incapable of furnishing a sequel to the death of Alcestis that would in any way resemble the sequel Euripides gives us, the restoration of the dead woman to life; and it is hardly less clearly incapable of so accounting for the presence of Helen in Egypt, and for Menelaus' belief that his wife had been with him from the fall of Troy to his landing on the Egyptian coast, as to leave the first part of the *Helena* essentially unchanged. Yet even in these two plays, all that is most interesting and significant in the character and behaviour of the human persons might remain unchanged, even if the story were made to end quite differently in the one play, and to begin quite differently in the other, instead of its remaining, as in other plays it might easily remain, from first to last substantially what it was before. A little reflexion on the content of the two plays should be enough to make the reader agree with this judgement, which it is therefore needless to defend by any critical analysis of the plays from the point of view of their human interest. But it may be observed that each of these two plays has a special character of its own which it is worth while to remember in the present connexion.

The *Alcestis* is a short play, and was performed the last of four, in the place of the more usual satyr drama. It is indeed something very different from a satyr drama; yet the last scene of it, hurried through in a perfunctory fashion that Verrall rightly calls unworthy of the ostensible subject, and marked by a levity, almost a frivolity of tone, that we find in no other tragedy, suggests at least a kinship with satyr drama. We can hardly be meant to take this scene seriously; the serious interest of the play is over by the time we reach this hasty winding-up of the story. Yet it is here, and here only, that supernatural causation occurs, unless we consider the death of Alcestis itself miraculous because it occurs on the day predicted by the oracle; but even so, the human interest of what precedes and follows it is what it would have been if the death had been purely natural. Further, the prologue, the debate (if it deserves such a name) between Apollo and Thanatos, is so wanting in gravity and impressiveness—as, once more, Verrall rightly says—that no allowance for the conventions of tragic form can prevent our feeling it below the dignity of tragedy: it reminds us far less of any other tragedy than of the *Ichneutae* or the *Cyclops*. The play is, in effect, a tragedy with a satyric prologue and finale; the human interest is all in the part that is tragedy, and would have been the same if the play had been so written, and its story so changed, that it was tragedy throughout.

The *Helena*, as has often been remarked, is from beginning to end less a tragedy, in any true sense, than a romantic melodrama: the outward guise of tragic form is preserved, but the inner substance of tragedy is wanting. Its human interest is not, as in the *Alcestis*, confined to a part of the play: it is evenly distributed throughout the whole. But the quality of that interest, which in the *Alcestis* is not below that of any other tragedy, is in the *Helena* on a much lower level; and even if the supernatural element, because unreplaceable by a natural equivalent, prevented our taking the human interest seriously, it would only prevent our doing what would in any case be difficult, and what very probably Euripides neither wished nor expected his audience to do. Whatever may be thought true of other plays, the feeling that 'things could not have occurred thus' is not likely to lessen anyone's enjoyment or understanding of the *Helena*.

We may fairly conclude then, that neither the *Alcestis* nor the *Helena* constitutes a real exception to the general principle stated, namely, that the human interest of those tragedies whose plots depend on supernatural causation is not destroyed by the consequent impossibility of the plot as a whole, because it is so easy to imagine the substitution of natural for supernatural causation, and therewith a possible for an impossible plot, with little or no change in the human story.

Having now stated my theory, and tried to answer some objections that might be brought against it at the outset, I must now support it by arguments of a more positive and constructive kind. Thus far, I have been maintaining not so much that it is sound as that some apparent reasons for thinking it unsound are not valid. We must now go further; and perhaps the next point to be argued is that the problem which the theory is intended to solve is not trivial or even imaginary, but both real and serious. This proposition I have as yet assumed, not proved. It is not, indeed, capable of being proved exactly and unanswerably. But it is fair to say that the existence of the problem, if not its gravity, has been recognized more or less clearly by most students of Euripides. There is the less reason to enlarge upon its nature, at this point, because this has been done by more than one writer with a precision and fullness on which it would be hard to improve. In particular Decharme, in the first three chapters of his well-known book *Euripides and the spirit of his dramas*, gives us a full and accurate account of what is known or may be confidently inferred about the poet's religious and philosophical views. These views amount to a semi-pantheism which is perhaps compatible with quite strong religious feeling, but regarded as theological dogma is not far removed from atheism, and is very far removed from any genuine belief in the anthropomorphic deities of the Olympian tradition. In so far, therefore, as Euripides causes such deities to play an active part in his dramas, he is presenting us with something in which he does not himself believe, depicting events which in his opinion did not happen, and could not have happened as he has deliberately shown them happening. The problem raised by this fact is surely neither imaginary nor trivial.

It may be argued, and has been argued, that he could not help doing what he did. Disbelief in the orthodox religious tradition could not be expressed openly in the theatre of Dionysus; and yet the 'sacred history' afforded the only subject-matter permissible. All, therefore, that he could do was to make the best of what was, for him, a bad business: to accept, as cheerfully as he could, the limits imposed by law or custom, and within these limits to present those stories of human character and destiny which he was directly concerned to present and with which the 'sacred history' provided him abundantly.

But this is not what we find he has done. Instead of making the best of a bad business, it may more truly be said that he has made the worst of a bad business. Instead of so selecting from the great mass of available legend, and so handling what he selected, that the part played by the gods was reduced to a minimum, or even, as would sometimes be possible, eliminated altogether, he has brought them into the picture in every single play, always at least in the background, and often in the foreground. Instead of modifying, or concealing, or suppressing the intellectually more incredible details of the old stories, he has introduced them in their original crudity, and sometimes even stressed them. Instead of omitting or softening such details of the stories as must be morally repellent, he has included them, and has frequently drawn our attention to them. His attitude to the established traditions is, in fact, not acquiescence but hostility. If anyone is disposed to question this statement, Decharme's second chapter provides ample evidence to support it; my own later chapters will incidentally provide a good deal more. Every means at Euripides' disposal—not only the irony and innuendo for which he was famous even in his lifetime, and of which he was perhaps as great a master as any man that has ever lived, but also, though it was less often employed, the means of direct statement through the mouths of his human characters—every means, I would say, short of downright and continuous denunciation, was employed, not in one or two plays only, but to some extent at least in every play without exception,[1] to ridicule and discredit

---

[1] Decharme himself excepts the *Suppliants*: but in Chapter IV I have argued that this play is not to be excepted.

the old tales, so far as they concern the gods, and thus to assail the conception of the divine nature which belief in the old tales implies.

There are, as we have seen, more reasons than one for his being able to do this with no very great danger to himself of being prosecuted for impiety. It seems that on one occasion he was in fact prosecuted on such a charge. But the same thing had befallen Aeschylus, and might easily befall any man who had enemies; and we do not know that Euripides was condemned. The real risk which it might seem he ran was the risk of being condemned not by the law as a blasphemer but by public opinion as a bad artist. To the Greek mind a most essential quality of any work of art was coherence, consistency, organic unity. The popularity of Euripides' plays shows that they were not thought, even in his own lifetime, to lack this quality; and that popularity lasted, and increased, for a long while after his death. Yet how can a play be an organic unity, what coherence and consistency can it possess, when it represents a series of occurrences as actual—or at least possible—historical facts, and yet intimates that in the author's opinion such things do not, did not and could not happen?

The problem, then, is both real and serious; and what I have called the 'ordinary' view offers us no adequate solution. It begins, indeed, by assuming the truth of what I myself believe true: namely, that the surface meaning of the play is its only meaning, so far as concerns the divine personages and supernatural events not less than so far as concerns the human personages and natural events. We are not to understand the gods as personifications of natural forces, but as persons; and we are not to disregard them as mere theatrical conventions, but to take them, their will and their power, as real causes of the events they are depicted as causing. So far so good. But when we ask 'What then are we to make of the poet's expressed unbelief in, and hostility towards, the received traditions implied and embodied in his plays?' the ordinary view has no satisfactory reply to give. Forbidden to ignore this unbelief and hostility, and unable to deny their existence altogether, it tends to belittle their extent and their importance, excusing them as unavoidable in so far as they do appear and do matter, and admitting, with more or less reluctance, that they constitute a real blemish on the excellence of the plays as works of art. But they were not unavoidable; they were not avoided; and we have no reason to think that any ancient critic thought that they injured the artistic excellence of the plays.

From these particular defects of the 'ordinary' view the 'rationalist' and 'symbolist' views are free. They neither ignore the problem nor belittle its gravity; and they are fully compatible with as high an estimate of the artistic merits of Euripides as his most fervent admirers could desire. They deserve, therefore, and shall receive, candid and careful consideration. No reasonable *a priori* objection can be taken to what is, broadly speaking, common to them both, as against the 'ordinary' view: namely, that the plays mean, in their supernatural aspects, something other than their literal and immediately obvious meaning. This is not, in itself, at all improbable. The only ground I find for rejecting either view is that, when applied to the actual facts of the plays as we read them, they do not appear to fit those facts: that while Euripides might well have written plays of which one view or the other would be the right one, he has not actually done so. In my second and third chapters I attempt a fair statement of these views, followed by my reasons for rejecting them, and for preferring the 'fantasy' theory as a solution of the main problem before us. Either of these views, if only it were true, would solve the problem; but for various reasons I must regard neither view as tenable. On the other hand, what I call the ordinary view is untenable just because it fails to solve the problem; and it is my immediate business to argue that my own view does at least offer an adequate solution: that it allows us to take the plays as we find them, and yet to recognize Euripides as both a great artist and also a religious heretic and satirist.

There is indeed one conceivable way out of the particular difficulty which the ordinary view seems to involve. I have said that this view tends to belittle the extent and importance of Euripides' hostility to the received religious tradition. There is one method of doing so which is both plausible and not uncommon, and which therefore deserves some special attention: namely, to assert that the heterodox opinions expressed or implied by personages in the plays are not the poet's own, or at least that we cannot be sure they are his. He is fond of presenting the arguments for or against this or that proposition concerning matters that were the subject of active interest and controversy in the Greece, and especially in the Athens, of his own day; and he presents these arguments so impartially, and refrains so completely from pronouncing judgement upon them, that we really cannot tell what he himself thinks. If, therefore, he has any purpose, in doing so, other than a tragic poet's natural purpose of embodying in his plays what is dramatically suitable and effective, this other purpose cannot be the propagation of any particular opinions. If it were so, he would take pains to make the arguments supporting those opinions appear to triumph over the opposing arguments. Instead of this, he seems rather to aim at placing before us the arguments on both sides, and leaving us to judge for ourselves between them. Why, it is asked, may this not be, in the particular matter of religion, a sufficient explanation of the heterodox sentiments which he now and then makes his personages express? Why must we attribute them to himself? Just as in all other matters his human personages are not idealized, but are, in essence, contemporary Greeks in their characters, feelings and beliefs, so too in this matter of religion. The heretic, even the atheist, was not unfamiliar in actual life, and within certain limits was free to express his views, if he wished to. He was therefore entitled to his place in the dramas of Euripides, and to him as to others a place is accorded. Whether Euripides himself was or was not a heretic or even an atheist, he has in this respect done only what might equally well have been done by the most orthodox of playwrights who shared his taste for depicting realistically, within the framework of ancient history and the conventions of tragic form, the life and thought of his own day.

To this line of argument I would reply, in the first place, that even where the controversial topic has nothing to do with religion, Euripides is not always impartial, nor his own judgement always incapable of being detected. That this is sometimes so, especially when the issue is of minor importance, may be admitted. A fair instance of this may be the debate in the *Heracles* (ll. 157–64, 188–203) between Lycus and Amphitryon on the respective merits of archer and hoplite. But it is otherwise, for instance, with the debate in the *Suppliants* (ll. 403–55) between Theseus and the Theban herald on the respective merits of tyranny and democracy. In this passage, if I am right, Euripides satirizes the shallowness and weakness of current Athenian arguments against the one form of government and in favour of the other. Here at least he reveals something of his own opinions to those who are ready and able to see what he is driving at. The same, I believe, is true of many other passages. If so, it may well be true of some or all of the passages dealing with religion; and we must not assume lightly that Euripides, in such places, is merely reproducing this or that bit of current controversy with no critical or propagandist purpose.

In the second place, religious questions are not handled in the same formal manner as many others are. We have no set debates on such topics: none, at least, on major issues, and none that are not immediately and clearly relevant (as in the *Bacchae*) to the dramatic needs of the play. The supreme issue, 'Do the Olympian gods exist, or do they not? and are they, or are they not, what tradition represents them as being?'—this issue cannot be a matter of formal debate in plays that assume, and must assume, on the surface anyhow, the affirmative answer. If the poet's own view is the negative one, and if he desires to indicate that view and to urge its truth, he cannot, in general, do so openly and directly. It might or might not be dangerous; but it must be prohibited, in any case, by the simplest considerations of artistic propriety. This holds good not only of his disbelief in the traditional religion, but also of his own positive religious beliefs. It is hard to see how these could possibly be set forth formally and at full length. The utmost we can expect is a hint here and a hint there; and this is what we get.

It will be useful at this point to recall the passages that tell us something of what Euripides himself believed. They are not numerous; they are not very easy to interpret, in themselves; and since, with one important exception, they are fragments whose dramatic setting is unknown, we must be cautious in our use of them as evidence. But they do tell us something; and fortunately the most instructive passage of all comes in an extant play. This passage is Hecuba's famous prayer in the *Troades* (ll. 884–88):

ὦ γῆς ὄχημα κἀπὶ γῆς ἔχων ἔδραν,
ὅστις ποτ' εἶ σύ, δυστόπαστος εἰδέναι,
Ζεύς, εἴτ' ἀνάγκη φύσεος εἴτε νοῦς βροτῶν,
προσευξάμην σε· πάντα γὰρ δι' ἀψόφου
βαίνων κελεύθου κατὰ δίκην τὰ θνήτ' ἄγεις.

Menelaus, hearing her speak thus, very naturally asks:

τί δ' ἔστιν; εὐχὰς ὡς ἐκαίνισας θεῶν.

But Hecuba does not reply; and not one word of all that precedes or follows throws any light on an utterance remarkable in itself and astonishing in its context. No conceivable interpretation of it can make it dramatically appropriate either to the speaker or to the situation. That Hecuba should appeal at this point for divine help is natural: that the appeal should take the form it does is wholly unnatural. What is the explanation? I can think of one and one only: that for five lines the speaker is in effect not Hecuba but Euripides, and that Euripides is here revealing something of what he believes about God and his relation to the world.

What that belief is becomes fairly clear if we compare this passage with two fragments:

(i) 935 Nauck (from the *Antiope*?):

ὁρᾷς τὸν ὑψοῦ τόνδ' ἄπειρον αἰθέρα
καὶ γῆν πέριξ ἔχονθ' ὑγραῖς ἐν ἀγκάλαις;
τοῦτον νόμιζε Ζῆνα, τόνδ' ἡγοῦ θεόν.

(ii) 1007 Nauck (from what play is unknown):

ὁ νοῦς γὰρ ἡμῶν ἐστιν ἐν ἑκάστῳ θεός.

We cannot, of course, even guess the speaker or the situation, with regard to these fragments or to most others. But Lucian, who quotes the first (*Jupiter Tragoedus*, 41), goes a long way towards assuring us of its dramatic irrelevance, and of its value as evidence of Euripides' own belief, by the words with which he introduces it, καθ' ἑαυτὸν ὁπόταν ὁ Εὐριπίδης, μηδὲν ἐπειγούσης τῆς χρείας τῶν δραμάτων, τὰ δοκοῦντά οἱ λέγῃ, ἄκουσον αὐτοῦ τότε παρρησιαζομένου. And even for the second passage Cicero's words (*Tusculan Disputations*, I, xxvi, 65) carry the same implication: 'animus, ut ego dico, divinus, ut Euripides audet dicere, deus est.'

Taking the three passages together, we may infer the following doctrine: There is a supreme deity. This deity is, in some sense, identical with the clear air (αἰθήρ) which surrounds the earth. It (or he) possesses life and consciousness, purpose and power. It is the ultimate cause of both physical and mental events, which are (in the main) regular and inevitable (cf. ἀνάγκη φύσεος and κατὰ δίκην ἄγεις). The minds of men are not merely of the same nature as this deity, but are so many separate parts of it. Monotheism and Providence are suggested, or at least not excluded, but are not clearly implied.

A few other fragments, the contexts of which are equally unknown, add little to what these three passages offer us, but confirm more or less what we have learnt already. Fragments 869 and 911 repeat the identification of Zeus with αἰθήρ; and this is not contradicted by 491 (αἰθέρ' οἴκησιν Διός), 903 or 938, and still less by 836 (from the *Chrysippus*):

Γαῖα μεγίστη καὶ Διὸς αἰθήρ,
ὁ μὲν ἀνθρώπων καὶ θεῶν γενέτωρ...

which at once suggests the traditional Zeus who is father of gods and men.

All these indications of Euripides' creed do not, taken together, carry us very far; and we cannot know how much further, if at all, he might have carried us if he had chosen. But we are justified in feeling that we do know something of his positive belief, and that he has gone as far towards telling us what it is as considerations of dramatic propriety—and perhaps also as far as regard for his personal safety—allowed him to go. There is no need to show that he held this belief with any strong conviction, or that he thought the pursuit and discovery of truth about such matters a very important thing, for himself or for anyone else. It may have been so; besides being a poet and a dramatist, he may have been a philosopher, and even, in some sense, a propagandist philosopher. That this is not certainly true does not justify our declaring it certainly untrue. But what is certainly true, I hold, is that he had a creed of his own, and has thought it worth while to show us what sort of thing it was, as well as attacking what he held to be false and harmful in current orthodox religion.

The importance of this fact, if it is a fact, is twofold. It prevents our belittling the extent and gravity of the main problem as the ordinary view tends to do. But it does something more. It suggests one motive for the assault on current orthodoxy. There are minds to which the destruction of error seems desirable, and worth much effort, even when they have no truth to substitute for the error; and it may be that such was the mind of Euripides. But to most minds the enterprise must seem more desirable, and worth more effort, if there is truth of some sort to take the place of exploded falsehood. We are now perhaps justified in supposing that Euripides felt

23

thus—that he was encouraged in his attempt to discredit what was incredible by his believing that he had something credible to offer in place of it.

It will be useful at this point to say something about the general question of his motives in assailing orthodoxy. For there is yet another objection that may be urged against my theory, an objection that may also be urged, and indeed has been urged, against Verrall's 'rationalist' interpretations: namely, that we cannot assign any sufficient motive for the active hostility towards orthodoxy which Verrall attributes, and I follow him in attributing, to Euripides. No man, we are truly enough told, was persecuted, no man was made even mildly uncomfortable because of his unusual religious opinions, so long as he stopped short of the public and blatant expression of what either was or appeared to be complete atheism. There were no clear canons of orthodoxy, no set creeds, no verbally-inspired scriptures, no formulae devised or endorsed by religious experts to distinguish between falsehood and truth. And if there had been these, there was no ecclesiastical authority to exact any sort of conformity with them from anyone. Attendance at public worship was no more a profession of faith than attendance at a play or a concert today; and the observance of private rituals was a simple convention of good manners and good taste. Here was a body of ideas hallowed by long acceptance, glorified by literature and by visual art, intimately interwoven with the whole fabric of personal and national life; shifting and un-systematized, yet rich and vital; in its mental and moral effects, harmless at the worst, at the best a real source of beauty and goodness. What, we are asked, could make any man wish to destroy it, or even to find fault with it?

In reply to this line of argument, I would first point out that I am not bound to support my theory by demonstrating what Euripides' actual motives were. Fortunately; for of course this cannot be done. Only he himself could tell us this, and he has not told us: we have no autobiography of his, no letters like those of Plato, no direct statement, in any shape, of what he thought or why he behaved as he did. What can and should be done is to refute the contention that no probable motive can be assigned. If we can see what his motive or motives may well have been, we shall no longer argue that he cannot have attacked orthodoxy because there was nothing to make him attack it; if we still think that he did not attack it, at least it will not be for this reason that we think so.

In attempting to suggest motives, it is needless to dwell at length on the general character of the 'age of enlightenment' in which Euripides lived and wrote. It is enough to remember that for an ever-increasing number of persons ancient tradition was steadily losing its authority. About all things in heaven and earth, about every aspect of public and private life, we can see that judgements of fact and judgements of value alike, hitherto accepted as a matter of course, were being rejected as false, or at least required to 'give account of themselves', and no longer allowed to claim credence on the simple ground of general acceptance. It is probable that this process neither began so suddenly nor operated so powerfully for good or evil as is commonly supposed. But it is a fact that no one can deny; and no one can deny that it is reflected in every play of Euripides. Opinion begins to divide only when we go on to ask how far he actively sympathized with it, and was not merely interested in it as an observer of human life. My own reading of his plays convinces me of his active sympathy with it. That his contemporaries attributed this attitude to him is suggested (though, I admit, not conclusively proved) by the tradition of his personal friendship with Anaxagoras, by much that we find in Aristophanes, and by other pieces of external evidence: and contemporary opinion, on such a matter, is not likely to have been wholly mistaken. All the available evidence taken together is perhaps too weak to prove him an active 'modernist'; but it strongly supports this interpretation, as against the reverse one, of the internal evidence of the plays themselves. And all the evidence tends to show that his modernism was not confined to matters of religion, but embraced many other departments of thought and life.[1] The more we recognize this fact, the less we shall be able to suspect him of conservatism in matters of religion.

To be sure, a man may hold strong convictions on important matters, and yet may feel no strong desire that other men shall share them; or at least he may refrain, for one reason or another, from taking active steps to cause other men to share them; and Euripides may have been such a man. But this was not, so far as one can see, the way of the Greeks in general: those who had something to tell the world seldom shrank from telling it. In this connexion it is worth while to remember the work of Xenophanes. If we did not possess the fragments of the poem in which he assailed religious anthropomorphism, it might have been possible to argue that he could not have done so because no motive for his doing so is discoverable. But that he did so is beyond doubt. We can only guess his motives, but whatever

---

[1] This will be noted further in connexion with my interpretation of the *Suppliants* in Chapter IV.

they were, they may equally well have inspired Euripides. And Euripides was a tragic poet; the tragic poets were recognized teachers of wisdom and virtue; Euripides might well feel it not only his privilege but his duty to teach wisdom and virtue as he understood them.

Even with regard to purely theoretical truth and falsehood, it seems absurd to contend that he had no reason for wishing to advance such truth and to destroy such falsehood. That truth and knowledge are valuable for their own sake, and their attainment a chief end of man, is a principle which Aristotle was perhaps the first to formulate clearly. But some consciousness of it is implied in all the efforts of the early philosophers; and they showed, by setting down their views in writing, a desire to share with others the knowledge they thought they had themselves attained. A simple love of truth and hatred of error, in himself and in others, may well have moved Euripides to do his best to discredit a system of theological beliefs of whose falsehood he was certain, especially if he had something to take its place.

But even if its mere falsity seemed to him no sufficient reason for assailing it, and the direct or indirect promotion of truer conceptions not worth the trouble and possible risk involved, another motive may have operated with compelling force. The moral imperfection of the gods as represented in the 'sacred history' probably had, in the fifth century if not earlier, a harmful effect both on the ideals and on the actual conduct of their worshippers. By that time, ethical theory and ethical practice, in some respects and to some extent, had advanced beyond those of the earlier time in which the sacred history took shape. Much, therefore, of the sacred history, in spite of all that men like Aeschylus or Pindar did to purge it, remained an obstacle to moral progress;

or at least—and this is all that my argument requires—it may well have appeared so to a man like Euripides. It could be maintained, and perhaps was, that divine beings cannot properly be judged by human standards, and that human beings are bound, in morals as in other respects, by rules and restrictions that cannot bind the gods. But such an attitude was possible only to a naïve and unreflecting piety which was certainly no part of Euripides' nature. A famous passage in the *Heracles* (ll. 1314–21) shows that he was alive to the moral dangers arising from acceptance of the sacred history. Theseus there seeks to save his friend from utter despair by recounting the shameful deeds of the gods which they have committed with no sequel of remorse or misery, and by bidding him not set up for himself a standard of goodness higher than that which the gods are content to adopt. The orthodoxy of the argument is perhaps stressed by its being put into the mouth of the hero-king of Athens. Heracles, indeed, dismisses it as founded on a false conception of the gods' nature. But what does this show? That if you do take this view of the gods' nature, the practical inference is valid—and the moral consequences are revolting. The argument is, to be sure, used here only to dissuade from excessive remorse after evil has been done; but it is plainly at the service, in advance, of intending evil-doers. Pheidippides, in the *Clouds*, pleads the example of Zeus himself to justify his outrageous treatment of his father: his doing so is put down to the vicious training given by the Sophists, but of course—whether Aristophanes saw this or not—the evil lay in the religious tradition itself, not in the cleverness or argumentative skill with which the new training furnished its pupils. The arrival of the latter of course made the continued acceptance of the former all the more

dangerous for morality; and we can believe that
Euripides felt the time was past for the mildly purgative
measures of some of his predecessors and contemporaries,
and the time come to discredit and dethrone the sacred
history as a whole.

Another motive may be suggested, a motive quite
distinct from the wish to promote truth and the wish to
promote morality, though fully compatible with both of
these. It may be called an artistic motive, and described
—more or less in Verrall's words—as the wish to provide
intelligent and enlightened spectators and readers with
a witty and elegant entertainment. To attribute this
motive to Euripides we must suppose what we are fully
justified in supposing, not only that his views were in the
main what I have indicated above, but also that his
public included a certain number of persons acute
enough to detect his purpose, and enough in sympathy
with him to approve it as well as to enjoy the skill with
which he carried it out. We may also assume that his
public included a number of relatively slow-witted and
simple-minded persons who could not detect his
purpose, and over whose heads, as it were, he appealed
to those who could. The method of his appeal has been
described by Verrall, in *Euripides the Rationalist*, so fully,
and with so much wit and eloquence, that no sort of re-
statement of it need or should be attempted here.
Verrall, indeed, goes further than I can follow him in
taking an important part of the entertainment to arise
from the indication of the real story that underlies the
fiction presented; for I deny the existence of any such
real story. But even without this, a full measure of such
entertainment is provided by the subtle methods that
mark the fictitious and impossible character of this or
that ostensible fact, and undermine the very opinions

that seem, at first sight, to be endorsed and advocated. The pleasure of the sharp-witted in discerning the playwright's real meaning under the cloak of traditional correctness would be increased by the unsuspecting approval of the simple-minded, and by the uneasy suspicion of others, more wary or better informed, that not all was quite what it appeared to be. We should note that religion is only one of several subjects on which we find Euripides exercising his powers of irony and wit in this fashion: my account of the *Suppliants* in my fourth chapter will illustrate the use of those powers for other purposes than religious satire. But the nature of tragic plots made religion the most obvious and accessible subject, and this is probably one reason for its being the commonest.

To avoid misunderstanding, I will now say once more that, whatever Euripides' motives were, in all this side of his work, I do not hold, and indeed would most earnestly deny, that this side of his work was the most important. No less than Aeschylus or Sophocles he was before all things a true tragic poet, concerned to present true, moving and beautiful pictures of human character and human destiny. This was his chief purpose and his chief achievement; and the appreciation of this should be our own chief aim in studying him, and the chief source of the profit and delight that he can give us. That is why he is a far greater dramatist than, for instance, two writers with whom he has been compared, and from our present point of view usefully compared—Voltaire and Shaw. Both these are his equals or his superiors as brilliant wits, as penetrating satirists, as vigorous champions of truth and justice; but he can give us abundantly something greater which it is almost beyond their power to give us at all. None the less, our profit and delight will be impaired so long as we fail also to appreciate the subsidiary purpose that I have been seeking to define and describe. I have argued that this subsidiary purpose was not incompatible with the chief purpose. That it did no harm at all, that the unity and charm of the plays in no way suffered from the inter-weaving of purposes so diverse—this is more than I wish to assert, nor indeed does my particular thesis require any such assertion. But it is easy to overestimate the amount of harm done. We are likely to do so unless we remember that a Greek tragedy is not a modern realistic play; that it differs from such a modern play, not only in external form but also in spirit and purpose, far more than is commonly recognized; and that what might injure and even ruin such a modern play, as a work of art, may leave a Greek tragedy unharmed.

CHAPTER II

THE SYMBOLIST THEORY:
THE *HIPPOLYTUS* AND *BACCHAE*

I WILL now examine what I will call, conveniently if not accurately, the *symbolist* or *symbolic* interpretation of the divine persons whom Euripides includes among his *dramatis personae*. This interpretation it is not easy to formulate clearly; and in trying to give lucid expression to what its defenders often leave vague and obscure, I may well be unfair to their actual intentions. But I must make the attempt, at whatever risk of unfairness; and this for several reasons. The interpretation of which I speak is, in the first place, *prima facie* plausible. It is in harmony with much in Greek thought, popular and poetic and philosophic thought, about which we need feel no serious doubt; in particular, with much that we find in Plato. In the next place, it has been adopted, in a greater or less degree, by many of Euripides' readers and critics; and especially, perhaps, by those who have felt that Verrall's views, untenable in detail and as a whole, have raised questions that must be answered seriously and not dismissed with a laugh of contempt. Thirdly, while I believe it mistaken, I think it does recognize something that is both true and important in the thought of Euripides. Finally, it must, so far as it is still retained, prevent our understanding one side of his work in what I take to be the right fashion.

Its essence may be expressed briefly, in the words of a recent writer, by saying that the gods of Euripides

THE SYMBOLIST THEORY

represent forces of nature or of the human soul.[1] We need
hardly, for our present purpose, consider gods that
represent the forces of purely physical nature—rain,
thunder, lightning, earthquake and the like; nor need
we consider very seriously those that represent the more
physical forces of human nature—life, growth, disease,
madness, death. The former, on any interpretation, play
only an occasional and incidental part in the action of
the tragedies. The part played by the latter is, to be sure,
more important: Thanatos in the *Alcestis* and Lyssa in
the *Heracles* are actual *dramatis personae*; and not only
death but bodily and mental disease are conspicuous
elements in the stories of tragedy, and not least in
Euripidean tragedy. But the test cases, so to speak, in
the present connexion, are the gods who represent,
according to the theory now being examined, the passions, emotions, or impulses of the human soul.

Obvious examples of such gods are Artemis and
Aphrodite in the *Hippolytus*, and Dionysus in the *Bacchae*.
Artemis represents the impulse to asceticism and
chastity; Aphrodite the passion of love; Dionysus the
impulse to cast off the restraints of ordinary life and 'let
oneself go'. The working of one or other of these passions
and impulses, in conditions where they meet with
opposition, causes or helps to cause the destruction of
Hippolytus, Phaedra and Pentheus. It may well be, we
are told, that Euripides supposed these passions and
impulses to be not merely a part of the nature of each
individual man, but something greater and more
universal that operates from without upon each man's
soul; mysterious but real forces, in no way analogous to

[1] G. M. A. Grube, 'Dionysus in the *Bacchae*' in *Transactions of the
American Philological Association*, LXVI (1935), pp. 37–54. This paper
deserves careful consideration: it is an energetic exposition of the view
I am here discussing.

human beings themselves, but nevertheless such that they may fittingly enough be called gods.

This conception is not, indeed, alien to orthodox religion, nor incompatible with it. The Olympian deities were not merely superhuman persons. Each had his sphere or spheres of operation, his function or functions which he performed with the regularity of a natural law; and each was identified, in a way that our imaginations cannot easily grasp, with the thing or process for which he was, so to speak, responsible. Achelous is at once a person who inhabits the river and the actual river itself. Dionysus is not merely the son of Zeus and Semele: he is also the cause of—it may even be said that he is—the vine, the grape, the wine, the emotions in the human soul that drinking wine produces or encourages. The Greek god is all that the Roman *numen* is, as well as being what the Roman *numen* is not: he is at once a force and a person. As a person, he has gradually acquired all the diverse emotions and desires that make up the personality of a human being. The personified river-god is made to act as a man would act if he were given immortality and complete control of the river. Dionysus, as a person, displays the emotions of pleasure, ambition, jealousy, resentment and the like, of which all human beings must be capable, but which have nothing to do with the functional *numen* of grape and wine. A religion of pure *numina* can have no mythology; and so the ancient Romans had no stories to tell about their gods. Hellenic myths, whatever their origin, are tales not about *numina* but about supermen. But because the superman does not cease to be a *numen*, the tales about him, generally speaking, are based upon, and centre around, his functions as a *numen*. As a superman, Dionysus the son of Zeus and Semele crushes Pentheus for denying his divine birth and refusing him divine honours. But the divine honours are those due to the *numen* of wine—the drinking of wine, and the unrestrained revelry that wine-drinking causes or encourages. The fate of Pentheus is therefore, we are told, also to be regarded as the fate of the fanatical puritan, of the man who insists upon sobriety and self-control in himself and others—the fate that befalls such a man when he seeks to suppress the wine-drinking and revelry that appeal strongly to many other people. That both the passion of love and the violent rejection of that passion may, in certain circumstances, work havoc in the lives of men and women, few would deny; and it is these forces which, encountering each other, ruin Hippolytus and Phaedra, not merely the mutual jealousy and hostility of two superhuman persons called Aphrodite and Artemis.

We are to suppose, then, that Euripides allegorizes the old tales and makes them into the parables of human life which they have always been, in some measure, even to those who accept them as historically true in their simplest and most literal sense. It is therefore not only the rules and conventions of tragic poetry at Athens that cause him to present stories taken from the sacred history, and to include deities among the personages of his plays. This indeed he is, like all other tragic poets, obliged to do. But the obligation is not irksome, not a fetter from which he would gladly free himself if public opinion would let him do so. He perceives that the old stories are true to the facts of life, and afford him, as they afford other poets, ample and suitable material for the pictures of human character and human fortunes which he desires to paint. He does not believe that these stories are, or could be, literally true. He does not believe that the gods are personal beings; still less that they are

35

just such personal beings as the stories imply that they are. But taken as allegories, and in their broad outlines, the stories are true, and the gods are adequate symbols of that which is wholly real and vitally important in the lives of men.

The nature of this interpretation of the 'divine' element in Euripides may stand out more clearly if we observe that it is, in one respect, like that of Verrall. It refuses, as Verrall's refuses, to take the surface meaning of the plays as their real meaning—or, at any rate, as the whole of their real meaning. To a certain extent, and in a certain sense, it may be said to rationalize the surface meaning: that is, to substitute for this surface meaning another meaning, a meaning more in harmony with the moral and intellectual beliefs of the poet himself and of the more discerning among the spectators and readers of his plays. Its supporters, like Verrall, imply that the surface meaning could not be regarded, except by very simple-minded persons, as giving us a series of events that actually occurred or could have actually occurred. Assuming, like Verrall, and indeed (so far as I am aware) like everyone else, that each play, taken as a whole, does nevertheless present us with such a series of possible events, they adopt, as Verrall adopts, a line of interpretation that seems to agree with this assumption. Look below the surface, they tell us—as Verrall tells us—and you will find nothing that does not square with the accepted facts of human experience; but you *must* look below the surface. Euripides is not (as Verrall thinks he is) actively hostile to the religious beliefs of his race and age; but he does not himself accept them, as Sophocles seems to accept them, just as they stand in the traditional stories and are implied by those stories. Therefore he must have meant something other than what at first sight he appears to mean. That is a statement which the 'symbolical' interpreters must be as ready as Verrall to make.

But to note the likeness between the two theories at once recalls our attention to the difference between them. And it is at once obvious that the symbolical theory has in one respect the advantage of a plausibility that Verrall's lacks. It does not require us to ignore considerable portions of the text—to consider them, I mean, no real part at all of the action of the play, but 'mere theatrical and conventional pretence, contradictory to the sense of the poet and transparent to the instructed reader'.[1] The divine appearances, at the beginning or at the end of a play, or, as sometimes happens, in the course of it, may be taken as real, and the divine utterances as significant. Not, to be sure, real and significant in quite the same way as those of the human personages; for the divine personages are symbols, and the human ones are not. But real and significant none the less; they do not contradict the sense of the poet, but complete it; without them we should not fully understand what the play means. The prologue *ex machina* is not merely a convenient if clumsy and 'uninspiring' device for getting the play going; nor is the epilogue *ex machina* a similar device for winding it up. Both prologue and epilogue are integral parts of the whole. We must, indeed, interpret them rightly; but if we do this—and only if we do this—we shall interpret the whole play rightly. Now this attitude, it will be agreed, is *prima facie* more probable and more attractive than Verrall's. And I am so far in agreement with it that I hold, as it holds, that the divine action is an integral part of the whole, not a conventional excrescence; that it is to be explained,

---

[1] Verrall, *Euripides the Rationalist*, p. 214.

but not explained away. What seems amiss to me is the particular explanation offered.

The same is true of the divine appearances, and of other supernatural occurrences, in the body of the play. These are relatively rare: in general, the supernatural is confined to the prologue or epilogue or both. But sometimes it occurs—for example, in the *Heraclidae* and the *Suppliants*—'off stage', reported by messengers, in the course of the play; and sometimes, at any rate ostensibly, before our eyes, as in the *Heracles* and the *Bacchae*. Here, too, the symbolic theory is not, like Verrall's, forced to explain the supernatural out of existence. Since the underlying and not the surface meaning is what matters to the discerning spectator, the suspension of disbelief required from such a spectator in respect of the surface meaning is made with relative ease. If the gods themselves are symbols, their miraculous actions are also symbols; and it is no harder to accept the latter than the former, once their symbolic character is understood. And the advantage which the symbolic theory, in this particular matter, possesses over Verrall's theory is obvious when we remember the strange shifts to which Verrall has to resort, in the *Heracles* and *Bacchae*, to explain, or rather to explain away, the supernatural occurrences that are actually put before our eyes. It must be hard even for his most whole-hearted supporters to believe that the appearance of Iris and Lyssa, and the conversation between them, are nothing but a dream— or a waking hallucination—of the Chorus. I am constrained to agree, therefore, that the symbolic interpretation is correct, in this matter, and Verrall's wrong.

There is, however, another respect in which the initial advantage may seem to rest—and I believe does rest— with Verrall as against the symbolists. The emphasis laid by Euripides on the evil disposition and immoral conduct of the gods in the traditional stories would appear, at first sight, incompatible with the symbolic interpretation. The 'forces of nature and of the human soul', it may well be felt, if they are to be symbolized at all by quasi-human divine beings, must not be symbolized by beings whose character and conduct put them on a level well below that of an ordinary decent man. I do not mean by this that the gods must not be shown as normally indifferent or even hostile, in will and act, to the welfare and happiness of man. It would be an extreme pessimism that would regard the physical and psychical forces of the world as consistently tending to man's misery and destruction; but Euripides, who certainly did not take a light-hearted view of life, may conceivably have been, like Thomas Hardy, a pessimist of this sort; enough of one, at least, to make such an outlook the basis of his tragedies—tragedy being, after all, a picture of the terrible and disastrous in human life, not of its delightful and prosperous aspects. I do not think, indeed, that his pessimism did take this form. If it did, it is strange that no single passage can be found in the extant plays and fragments that expressly conveys such a belief; none, I think, that even suggests it dimly; whereas in Hardy's novels and poems it is expressed with the utmost clearness and with an almost wearisome reiteration. On the contrary, there are passages that seem to reject such a belief, to argue that it is the folly, or lust, or selfishness, of individual human beings that brings misery to themselves and to others. 'It was not Cypris,' says Hecuba to Helen, 'but your own heart, that made you yield to Paris':

ὁ σὸς δ' ἰδών νιν νοῦς ἐποιήθη Κύπρις...
(*Troades*, ll. 983–97).

The fault is not in our gods but in ourselves. We are responsible beings who can, if we will, choose the right and refuse the wrong. We are not the victims of external forces[1] that control our bodies or our souls; and the traditional tales that so represent us are not merely false but morally harmful. Some such view of life, a view which, however pessimistic, is the exact opposite of Hardy's, appears to me to be that which Euripides held. If I am right, the symbolic explanation of his picture of the gods at once becomes untenable; they are excluded, as natural forces, no less than as crudely anthropomorphic persons, from playing any significant part in the drama of human life.

But this is not the only objection to the symbolists' explanation. Even could they show that Euripides' philosophy of life was much like Hardy's, it would still be hard for them—I would say impossible—to account for the mean, paltry, contemptible moral character of the gods he puts on the stage. It is needless to argue at length with those who may be disposed to question the fact itself. They may be referred to the full and convincing exposition of it by Decharme (section 2 of his second chapter). It is almost enough to think of such outstanding cases as Hera in the *Heracles*, Aphrodite in the *Hippolytus*, and Apollo in the *Ion*. The behaviour of these persons, if attributed to human beings, would inevitably be felt despicable and loathsome. Nothing but the sheer force of religious tradition could procure the toleration of such behaviour when attributed to divine beings. The force of tradition can do much; it did much for Euripides; the hostility he aroused by his treatment of the gods may or may not have been con-

---

[1] This point is further argued, with further reference to the *Troades* passage, on p. 56.

40

siderable, it may or may not have deprived him of first prizes and endangered his personal safety, but at least he was never, so far as we know, condemned or punished for impiety. And so long as we look upon his stage gods as the personal beings of religious tradition, there is no artistic absurdity involved in their representation as persons of degraded and undignified character: the offence, if there is one, is not against art but against religion, and if religious sensibilities are not too deeply wounded, all is well; no other sensibilities need be so much as slightly jarred. But to personify the great cosmic forces of nature thus is quite another matter. If they are to be shown as men, they should be shown as supermen, and cannot possibly be shown as submen. That they should be cruel and terrible tyrants is at least conceivable: it is not even conceivable that a man of ordinary taste and understanding, to say nothing of a great poet and thinker, should make them into the meanest sort of knaves, cowards and fools, creatures whose leading motives are spite and jealousy, towards men and towards one another, and whose wisdom is, in some cases at least, no greater than their goodness. Decharme understates the truth when he says: 'Euripides is generally more disposed to point out the evil which the gods occasion to men than the good which may be attributed to them.' It would be a bold but hardly excessive generalization to say that the gods in Euripides neither do good nor are good except for their own advantage. (The chief apparent exception to this is offered by the *Suppliants*; but I hope to show in my fourth chapter that the spirit of this play has been totally misconceived, by Decharme as by everyone else.)

The above arguments are of so general a nature, and have in them so much of what may be considered an instinctive and perhaps prejudiced personal reaction to the agreed facts, that it will be well to reinforce them by applying them to one or more single plays. It will perhaps be granted that if the symbolical method of interpretation is valid for any of the plays, it must be valid for the *Hippolytus* and the *Bacchae*, and that in so far as it can be shown not to be valid for these plays its plausibility as a general principle of interpretation will be destroyed.

Into the story of the *Hippolytus*, as presented by Euripides, three divine persons enter. Of these, Aphrodite alone both appears and plays an active part; Artemis appears, but is not active; Poseidon is active, but does not appear. None the less, an adequate symbolical interpretation of the divine element in the play should provide for all three deities. Can it do so convincingly?

We may first consider Poseidon. His part in the story is confined to the production of the miraculous monster which makes the horses bolt and so causes the death of Hippolytus. The miracle is represented as a direct answer to the prayer of Theseus. It is hard to see how the symbolical principle of interpretation can be applied to this incident. Poseidon could of course represent the sea and all that is therein; his activity could represent that of the sea, or of any sea-creature. But how could the sea and its inhabitants be subject to the will of Theseus, so as to become the instrument of his vengeance? Yet something like this is what the symbolist theory requires. Either the incident is a pure accident, or it is not. To regard it as a pure accident is not to explain it, but to remove its connexion with the prayer of Theseus, and so to rob it of all significance. But if it is not a pure accident, what does it mean to the symbolist? To what possible sequence of natural events, psychical or physical or both, can the traditional story, as presented to us, correspond? No doubt it may be argued that symbolists are not bound to provide an answer to this question; that their line of interpretation is not required for every supernatural detail in every play, and need not be applied to the matter before us. This, however, is to admit that some other kind of interpretation is required here; and from this it would not be unfair to argue that a line of interpretation that can be applied to all cases of the supernatural is more likely to be the right one, in any given case, than one that can, at best, be applied to some cases only. It will not do to say that in the present case no particular interpretation of any kind is required; that we have here a romantic and moving part of the traditional story, 'good theatre', and therefore adopted by Euripides without any special consideration of its bearing on the rest of the plot. Admittedly it is 'good theatre', highly romantic, deeply moving. But it is more than this: its connexion with the rest of the plot is intimate, indeed vital. Unless it can be shown to mean something, it is worse than a casual and irrelevant excrescence: it reduces the story as a whole to hopeless confusion, to a sequence of unrelated events that can, as a whole, signify nothing at all.

Poseidon and his activities, then, present to the symbolists a difficulty which it is neither permissible for them to ignore nor easy for them to surmount. If it should nevertheless somehow be removed, would the way then be open for them to explain Aphrodite and Artemis as symbols of natural forces? Granted that Euripides does not merely believe in these deities as the glorified human persons of tradition, does he here present them, and intend them to be understood by all who can and will, as symbols of certain real and powerful human passions and instincts? Does Aphrodite simply represent the passion of love, and Artemis the craving for a chaste and ascetic life? And has the poet built up, on this basis, a tale whose tragic outcome is due, essentially, to the conflict of these instincts, a tale fully intelligible to persons who are as far as himself from any naïve acceptance of traditional theology? It must be admitted that he might well have given us a *Hippolytus* of this character; for this, *mutatis mutandis*, is the character of his *Medea*, and partly or wholly the character of several of his other plays, in which the gods are not represented as the 'moving causes' of what happens. Therefore it is not at the outset improbable that the *Hippolytus* also should be, at bottom, of this character, and that the symbolical employment of divine persons, while not, for easily conceivable reasons, found in those other plays, should for not less easily conceivable reasons be found in this one. Further, the play does show the passions and instincts in question possessing Phaedra and Hippolytus, and its human interest—which, let me say again, is the *chief* interest in *all* Euripides' plays—is primarily due to this fact. Notwithstanding this, the reasons for rejecting a purely symbolical interpretation of Aphrodite and Artemis are very strong. I will mention two such reasons. The first is based on the personal character of the two goddesses, as displayed by their own words in the prologue and epilogue. The second is based on the nature of the actual plot of the play.

On the first reason I will dwell less than on the second, not because I myself find it less convincing, but because it is less capable of convincing those whose general attitude predisposes them against it; also because it consists in applying to this play a general principle

44

already stated. If Aphrodite and Artemis are personified natural forces, they ought to be personified not as human but as superhuman persons; or if as human persons, at least as noble human persons. Pitiless they may be, but not malignant; evil, in a sense, they may be, but not mean and base. But, as I read their utterances in this play, malignant and mean and base is what they are. The callous cruelty of Aphrodite is that of a selfish jealous woman, who resents the devotion of a youth to another woman than herself, and has no scruple in revenging herself on him by ruining other innocent people as well: she tells us this in so many words. Artemis shows little pity for her devoted servant as he dies in torment; but she shows great resentment against Aphrodite, and a cold-blooded determination to get even with her by killing her own favourite. All this is intelligible enough as religious satire: it is a fair enough comment on the 'facts' of the legend, a fair enough statement of what the legend implies. But as a symbolic representation of the workings of natural forces in the lives of men it would be absurdly inappropriate, and therefore utterly misleading.

But it is the actual plot of the play that can most effectively be brought forward against the symbolists. If the play were only, or even mainly, concerned with the character and fate of Phaedra, their interpretation of Aphrodite would be more plausible. The passion of love has undoubtedly brought unhappiness, ruin and death to many. To attribute such disasters to the will of Aphrodite, even to exhibit the goddess herself declaring her intention of bringing them to pass, would be nothing very strange or remarkable—not more so than, for instance, the part played by Athena in the *Ajax* of Sophocles; and the story of Phaedra, if considered by itself, is from first to last wholly explicable without assuming the truth of anything that the most hardened atheist would not readily accept. But Phaedra's part in the play, important as it is, must yet be held to be of secondary importance. The leading figure, from every point of view, is not Phaedra but Hippolytus. It is his character, his conduct, his fate, not hers, upon which our chief interest is, or should be, concentrated. We are apt, perhaps, to overrate the importance of the 'heroine' in many Greek tragedies: Deianeira, for instance, at the expense of Heracles, and even Antigone at the expense of Creon. But we have little excuse for putting Phaedra even on the same level of importance as Hippolytus. She is the means to his ruin, not he to hers. Aphrodite makes this quite clear in the prologue: she all but regrets having to destroy Phaedra in order to destroy Hippolytus; would pity her, if she were capable of pity; but not being so, destroys her callously in order to achieve her primary purpose. The tragedy is the tragedy of Hippolytus; and if we consider carefully what Hippolytus is and does and suffers, the symbolical interpretation becomes, as I hope to show, impossible.

For, in order to make it possible, the story should run differently in one important respect: the fate of Hippolytus should be the result of his peculiar temperament, of his settled aversion from the pleasures of sexual love. It may be objected that this is just what happens: that the indignant horror with which he rejects what he supposes to be Phaedra's advances is the direct cause of the disastrous sequel, and that his peculiar temperament is the direct cause of his indignant horror. Now while the first of these two statements is certainly true, the second is not. It is not the peculiar temperament of Hippolytus, but his upright moral character, to which

46

his indignant horror is due. Union with his father's wife would be both adulterous and incestuous; and all respectable Greeks, whatever their attitude to religion, regarded both adultery and incest as horrible offences. If this required proof, the *Oedipus Tyrannus* would prove it; but we need not go beyond the *Hippolytus* itself; we have only to think of Phaedra's desperate shame and misery while her secret is still unrevealed, and the horror even of the much less scrupulous nurse when she first learns the truth. The most amorously-disposed of Greek youths could scarcely, unless he were a hardened reprobate, feel and speak less strongly than Hippolytus feels and speaks upon learning—as he supposes—that his stepmother desires to lie with him in his father's bed. Only a hardened reprobate, therefore, in the story as we have it, could escape the fate that befalls Hippolytus. It is the upright character of Hippolytus, I repeat, not his peculiar temperament, that brings his fate upon him. To the story as taken at its face value, the peculiarity of his temperament is not merely relevant, but essential: it is precisely this which arouses Aphrodite's resentment. But to the story as symbolically interpreted, it is not only not essential, but not even relevant in the smallest degree. Such a temperament may, to be sure, strike us as something strained, unhealthy, unnatural; and we may, though perhaps not very easily, conceive of a play that would, symbolically interpreted, display it as leading to some moral or physical disaster. If we imagine such a youth as Hippolytus rejecting with scorn the offer of a love that he might have accepted without guilt, and then the scorned woman taking her revenge by causing his death, we have a plot that would at least be capable of such treatment as might justify the symbolic method of interpretation. However, such speculations are

47

beside the purpose; for this is not what the plot of the *Hippolytus* is. If we take the play as we have it, we may suppose, if we will, that Euripides intends his hero's disposition to be thought of as strained and unhealthy and unnatural. But so long as it is not this disposition, but the normal conduct of an ordinary decent man, that brings him to his doom, the only 'moral' that can be drawn from the play is the one which I feel sure Euripides intended: namely, that the traditional story, with its callous, jealous, revengeful deities, is intellectually incredible and morally repulsive.

To avoid misunderstanding, let me add that I do not suppose this 'moral' to constitute the only, or even the chief, significance of the play. I am not only ready to admit, but eager to assert, the full contrary. In the *Hippolytus*, as in all other plays where the element of religious satire occurs, that element is altogether subordinate to the poet's main purpose. But there is no need to develop, in this special connexion, an argument that has already been set forth in my first chapter.

Let us turn, with the same caveat against the same misunderstanding, to examine the possibility of applying the symbolic principle of interpretation to the *Bacchae*. Once this principle has been shown not to be applicable to the *Hippolytus*, we shall be less inclined to think it probably applicable to the *Bacchae*, or to any other play. Still, it may be so. On any showing, the *Bacchae* is a remarkable and mysterious piece of work, and it may well be that the right principle for its interpretation is one that would be wrong for anything else in Euripides.

We may begin our examination of it by ruling out from our present consideration certain views of it that have been held, and are more or less plausible, but are no necessary part of any symbolic interpretation, and would

48

probably not be held by most symbolists. One such view is that it embodies a recantation, partial or complete, of Euripides' active hostility to religious orthodoxy in general. Another is the rationalist view held by Verrall, which eliminates altogether the supernatural and miraculous, ignoring the Dionysus of the prologue and epilogue as a mere theatrical convention which the enlightened are not to take seriously, and explaining the Dionysus of the body of the play as really a man and not a god in human shape. Both these views deserve examination; but neither need be examined, unless incidentally, for our present purpose.

A symbolic interpretation of the *Bacchae*, whatever it does or does not include, must at least assert this: that Euripides shows us the conflict of two incompatible human instincts or tendencies, and the victory of one over the other. Just as in the *Hippolytus* the passion of love comes into inevitably disastrous conflict with the passionate desire for chastity, so in the *Bacchae* the instinct prompting to reckless self-indulgence, 'letting oneself go', comes into inevitably disastrous conflict with the instinct prompting to careful self-restraint, 'holding oneself in'. Dionysus symbolizes the former instinct: the latter has no specific divine symbol. Thus Dionysus corresponds to Aphrodite in the *Hippolytus*, but we have no deity in the *Bacchae* to correspond to Artemis. The orgiastic worship of Dionysus stands for the gratification of the former instinct: the refusal of that worship, and the attempt to suppress it, for the gratification of the latter. On so much as this, surely, the supporters of any symbolic interpretation must be agreed.

When, however, we ask what the 'moral' of the play is, on which side the poet's sympathies lie, this agreement may cease. For three different answers may be given to this question, all of them compatible with the symbolic principle of interpretation. The 'moral' may be (i) that the Dionysiac element in life is good and desirable, and any attempt to suppress it is wrong; (ii) that it is bad, and ought to be suppressed, by force if necessary; (iii) that it is neither very good nor very bad, and its attempted suppression is neither a noble nor a wicked act. Since attempted suppression is bound to fail disastrously, human life, so far as this matter is concerned, will correspondingly be conceived of as ruled (i) by justice, (ii) by injustice, or (iii) by neither; and Pentheus, who embodies the anti-Dionysiac instinct, must be regarded (i) as the villain of the piece, (ii) as a martyr in a good cause, or (iii) as neither, but simply as the victim of an unfortunate state of affairs that is part of the inevitable evil of the world as we know it. A symbolical interpretation of the play will accordingly take some one of three corresponding forms: it will be convenient to speak of the first, second and third interpretations. Of the three, I believe that the second comes nearest the truth, that nevertheless it cannot be maintained successfully, and that the first and third are even less tenable. As in the *Hippolytus*, the arguments against them are twofold: one group is based on the character of Dionysus, the other on the nature of the actual plot of the play.

The character of Dionysus in the *Bacchae* is so much like that of Aphrodite in the *Hippolytus* that almost the same words as before might be used to show his unfitness to symbolize the beauty and joy of which his worshippers, in the lovely choruses, have so much to say. It is not merely that he is diabolically cruel throughout: admittedly so in the second half of the play, and not less so, as it appears to me, in the first half. For it might be argued that forces of nature are, if not cruel, at least ruthless; and though the lack of benevolence is not the same thing as positive malevolence, yet the latter, in a quasi-human being, might in certain circumstances symbolize well enough the passionless indifference to human welfare of a natural force. Not that even this line of argument will stand close examination. The natural force which Dionysus must represent, if he represents any such thing, is not a purely physical force, not a force wholly external to man, like lightning or storm or pestilence. It is a psychical force, an instinct of the human spirit, something whose whole meaning is bound up with the happiness and welfare of man. The Dionysiac gospel is a gospel of freedom and joy, or it is nothing. If it is a true gospel, its rejection means loss: those who reject it miss a freedom and a joy that might have been theirs. For such persons the preachers of the gospel may feel pity, perhaps also contempt; but what room is there for them to feel even resentment, let alone the desire for a cruel and unsparing vengeance, for a vengeance that involves, moreover, the innocent in the ruin of the guilty? Not, however, to press this point further, we may ask what the motive for Dionysus' cruelty is; and we find, as we found with Aphrodite, that it is a mean motive. Dionysus is determined to exact from Thebes a full recognition of his divinity; he will at all costs be honoured and worshipped; if not by willing worshippers, then by unwilling ones. He is a self-seeking egoist of the basest type. It is absurd to speak of his patience and courage under the insults and persecutions of Pentheus, as if he were really the human being he pretends to be. One might as well attribute patience and courage to the cat playing with the mouse. Not only is this god a devil, but he is not even a noble devil. He should at least be a noble devil to justify even the second interpretation of the three: to justify either of the others, he should not even be a devil, still less be an ignoble one. But enough of this line of reasoning, which can never appear completely cogent to those who are predisposed against the conclusions to which it leads. It is from the actual plot of the play, as with the *Hippolytus*, that the inadequacy of the symbolic principle of interpretation can be most convincingly demonstrated.

First, let us notice what the fundamental ground of quarrel between Dionysus and his Theban opponents is. It is the question of the paternity of Semele's son. The 'truth' is that Zeus is his father. This account of the matter, maintained by Semele herself and accepted by her father Cadmus, has been rejected by her sisters, and by her nephew King Pentheus. They hold that Semele, having been seduced by some mortal man, tried to conceal her 'error' by claiming Zeus as her lover, and that she was instigated to this course by her father. Their belief has been confirmed by the fact that Semele was struck by lightning and killed as she was giving birth to her child. This, the prologue informs us, was really the act of the jealous and resentful Hera; but they attribute it to Zeus, who thus punished Semele for her blasphemous falsehood. At some unspecified time after this event, a band of Asiatic women, led by a Lydian youth, arrives at Thebes, proclaiming the son of Semele to be the son of Zeus, and urging the Thebans to believe in him, and to join in the orgies that are at once the result of his inspiration and the recognized way of worshipping him. Not unnaturally, the king and his people refuse to believe the story, or to adopt the religious observances of which belief in the story is obviously a necessary condition. Dionysus' anger is aroused primarily because of their disbelief. Before all things he is resolved to prove himself the son of Zeus. We know this, because he has told us so. But Pentheus and the Thebans have no such means of learning the truth. The goodness or badness of the cult is not, at the outset, the main issue. If we look carefully at what Pentheus says in his first speech (ll. 215–62), we do not find him condemning the cult itself. He might well do so. It is a foreign cult, not yet practised anywhere in Greece (see l. 20): on that ground alone it might well be regarded as, to say the least of it, unsuited to form part of the religious practice of a Greek community. But the king does not attack it on that ground or on any other. He does not even deny the divinity of 'this mysterious new deity Dionysus'. What he does say is that the Lydian youth is a charlatan and a seducer; that the women of Thebes, perverted by this youth, are not genuine worshippers of Dionysus, but are making the new rites an excuse for wholesale drunkenness and sexual licence; and that the new god is at any rate not the child of Semele, for that child was killed at birth by the lightning flash that killed his mother. That Pentheus is mistaken in all these statements the hideous sequel proves, at least so as to convince the surviving victims of the angry god. But to the question of whether the cult of Dionysus is a good or a bad thing, whether the periodical abandonment of the traditional σωφροσύνη for outbursts of ἀκολασία under the aegis of religion is or is not a necessary part of a well-balanced and healthy life—to this question the sequel is wholly irrelevant. It is irrelevant on any of the three interpretations: not less irrelevant if Dionysus be taken, according to the second interpretation, as symbolizing a maleficent and destructive force of nature, than if he be taken, according to the first, as a beneficent and constructive one. We do not, therefore, escape the difficulties of a symbolic interpretation by refusing—as

53

I feel sure, for many reasons, we must refuse—to agree with Professor Grube in regarding Pentheus as a prurient puritan, the mentally-diseased exponent and would-be enforcer of a lop-sided and unwholesome morality.

These difficulties are not lessened if we take into account the misery that befalls Cadmus and his daughters. That the guilty, or even the merely mis-guided, may involve innocent and right-minded persons in their own ruin is a sad but undeniable fact of human life. But the play represents Cadmus and his daughters as punished for misdeeds of their own. This they them-selves confess, even while they protest against the merciless severity of their punishment. Yet what were these misdeeds? The daughters had not abstained from joining in the worship of Dionysus. That the god has forced them to join in it against their wills, that they had resisted the Bacchic frenzy to which other votaries had gladly submitted themselves, is nowhere stated and nowhere clearly implied. Their wrongdoing was intellectual, and even within this sphere limited to a single error. It is not really true that they had rejected the god Dionysus: what they rejected was the story of his birth proclaimed by his devotees; they refused to believe in the divine fatherhood of Semele's son, and therefore in *that son's* divinity and power. Cadmus both accepted that belief and joined willingly in the worship. He, at least, should be wholly guiltless even in the sight of Dionysus himself. The utmost that can be said against him is that he counsels Pentheus (ll. 333–6) to an in-sincere acceptance of the belief if he finds sincere accep-tance impossible, advice which no Greek would understand as indicating insincerity in Cadmus himself. Thus the misdeeds of the god's other victims, whether real or imaginary, have nothing to do with the meaning

54

or value of the Bacchic orgies. They are purely theological sins, concerned solely with what we are constantly told (though, I feel sure, wrongly told) is a quite subsidiary and unimportant part of Greek religion, namely, intellectual belief as opposed to external observance of rites and ceremonies. There can be little need to enlarge on the unsuitableness of all this for any symbolic interpretation of the play as representing the disastrous conflict of two deeply-seated instincts of human nature.

After all this, it may still be thought—and indeed the suggestion has been made to me—that there is still *some* room left for a symbolist interpretation of the deities in these two plays. It may be thought that, even if the representation of these deities is what I have sought to show that it is, yet this is not the whole truth of the matter. Must Aphrodite and Artemis and Dionysus, in these plays, be *either* incredible and repulsive fictions *or* real powers in human life? Can they not, in some sense, be both? Can they not, in some measure, stand for, represent, symbolize, the dispositions and emotions and passions which are commonly associated with their names, and which do most clearly and potently possess and control the human personages of the plays? If Euripides regularly attempts two things at once, satire and poetic drama, may he not be attempting them in this particular way among others? And if he is, then do not these two plays, at least, deserve to be regarded as something better than incredible fictions? No such argument, to be sure, will serve for the *Alcestis, Iphigenia in Tauris, Ion* or *Helena*. But these are plays of a different sort, and it is quite arguable that the divine personages and activities in them are not of the same order. At any rate, in the *Hippolytus* and *Bacchae* we see sexual love, the desire for chastity and the desire for reckless revelry laying hold of human beings, in a quite natural and familiar way though with exceptional and terrible results. Do not the words and behaviour of the deities concerned to some extent symbolize these realities of human experience?

Now while my general thesis, in this chapter and in this book as a whole, would not be seriously weakened by the acceptance of this suggestion, there is perhaps good reason for not going even so far as this. Let us ask ourselves the following question: What, in Euripides' view, is the cause or source of human dispositions and emotions and passions? Does he think of these as due to mysterious but very real powers or agencies which are external to men, which take possession of them, wholly or partially, permanently or intermittently, from without? Or does he think of them as inherent in men, as no less a natural part of men than the bodily limbs and organs, subject to outside agencies only in the sense in which minds and bodies alike are subject, like everything else, to the great governing power, Zeus, aether, mind, that directs the universe?

It would be rash to answer this question confidently on the strength of a single line or two from one play; yet there is at least one famous passage which is enough by itself to show that the latter answer may be the right one. In the *Troades*, Helen defends her conduct by making herself out to have been the helpless victim of Aphrodite: Hecuba rejects this plea, and declares that the beauty of Paris, and the prospect of wealth and luxury with him in Troy, made Helen choose quite deliberately to go off with him.

ἦν οὑμὸς υἱὸς κάλλος εὐπρεπέστατος,
ὁ σὸς δ' ἰδών νιν νοῦς ἐποιήθη Κύπρις·
τὰ μῶρα γὰρ πάντ' ἐστὶν 'Αφροδίτη βροτοῖς,
καὶ τοὔνομ' ἐρῶς ἀφροσύνης ἄρχει θεᾶς.

(*Troades*, ll. 987–90.)

That Hecuba should be made to speak thus shows clearly that to Euripides the latter of the above explanations of human passions may well have seemed the natural and right one. He may well have thought that, though men's behaviour of course depends in part on the influence which other persons and external circumstances have on their passions and emotions, yet these passions and emotions are part of themselves, not something imposed from without. No accumulation of expressions seeming to point the other way can disprove this: we commonly today talk of being seized by a great thirst or a violent desire, without having the smallest tendency to think of thirst or desire as external powers. There is nothing to show that Euripides did not take this second view; and if he did, then what powers, what external agencies of any kind, can Aphrodite and Artemis and Dionysus stand for? However mysterious the springs of feeling and action may be, if they rise within us they do not pour into us from without. In so far as this line of reasoning seems valid, it will tell against accepting even a modified symbolist explanation of Dionysus and the rest. And if it should be impatiently rejoined that poetry is one thing and scientific psychology quite another, and that Euripides was perhaps a philosopher but was certainly a poet—well, does not the burden of proof rest on those who would deny the uniform consistency of his thought about such matters, and not on those who would affirm it?

My treatment of the *Hippolytus* and the *Bacchae* in this chapter should not be taken as pretending to be a full discussion of these plays, even from the special point of view with which this book is chiefly concerned. Much more would be needed to set forth adequately my interpretation of them as 'fantasies', as presentations of series

57

of events which, taken as a whole, could not have occurred. Here, as in other plays, the human personages are not idealized, but are depicted, within the limits imposed by the conventions of tragic form, realistically; and the divine personages are represented as the received stories implied, in Euripides' opinion, that they ought to be represented, namely, as superhuman beings, superior to men in power, but inferior to men morally and even intellectually. Here as elsewhere we are shown what might have occurred, or even must have occurred, *if* the received stories were true, and yet cannot have occurred, because the received stories are not true and cannot be true. And here as elsewhere we perceive that one of the poet's purposes—not the sole one, not the main one, but still one among others—is to satirize the orthodox beliefs of his day. Much more, I repeat, than has been said is needed to justify this interpretation of these two plays; and much more still would be needed to provide a complete and balanced account of their meaning and value as wholes. The latter task is not even attempted in this book; and the present chapter is merely a contribution to the former task, offering a merely negative argument, seeking simply to discredit a principle of interpretation which, in so far as it is accepted, must prevent the acceptance of the 'fantasy' theory which I am chiefly concerned to establish. Let me say again, in conclusion, that if symbolic interpretation will not fit the *Hippolytus* and the *Bacchae*, there is no play of Euripides which it can possibly fit; and that, since there are some plays which it cannot possibly fit in any case, it is for that reason less likely to be the right one even where, as with these two plays, it is not at once obvious that it is the wrong one.

CHAPTER III

THE RATIONALIST THEORY: THE *HERACLES*

In this chapter it is my purpose to examine the solution of our problem offered by what I have called the rationalist theory. Verrall has convinced some students of Greek tragedy that this interpretation of Euripides is the right one. They accept his general theory, and also his particular treatment of the eight plays which he discussed fully. They may doubt, or even reject, this or that detail of his argument; but they feel sure he is right in the main. It would be interesting, if it were possible, to learn what proportion of his readers he has convinced. The proportion is perhaps quite a small one. But it is large enough not to be negligible; and it deserves special consideration from anyone who holds, as I do, not only that one part of Verrall's theory is true and important, but also that the other part, though not true, is not *a priori* absurd or even improbable, and that it can be disproved only by showing that the actual reasons he gave for maintaining it are not valid. It therefore seems proper to examine the whole of his case in connexion with at least one of the plays which he handled at length. Let us, for this purpose, take his account of the *Heracles*:[1] not that, for this purpose, his account of any of the other seven plays would, in most respects, serve less well; but the *Heracles* will serve at least as well as any other.

[1] *Four Plays of Euripides*, pp. 134–98.

The ostensible story of this play is, according to Verrall, not the real one; and the real one is briefly this. Heracles is, like other men, the son of a human father. He is a man of exceptional strength and courage, who has performed many wonderful and beneficent deeds of valour. But none of these involve the miraculous. A lion, a boar, a bull, he may well have killed; but the hydra, the three-headed giant, and such monsters, are the inventions or exaggerations of superstition. So, too, is the belief that he is the son of Zeus, and strangled in his cradle the serpents Hera sent to destroy him. These superstitious beliefs arose first in the minds of other people; but he has come to share in them himself. For he is like some other great heroes in having an 'unbalanced' temperament. The circumstances engender in him what may be called megalomania; and this, if he is subjected to an exceptional emotional strain, may easily topple him over into madness. Returning home from an adventure in some underground cavern, which has led himself as well as other people to fancy he has been in the kingdom of the dead, he finds his father and wife and children in immediate danger of death at the hands of an usurping tyrant. He kills the tyrant, and saves his family. But the emotional strain, which is certainly exceptional, is too much for his sanity. A frenzied madness seizes him; he kills his wife and children, and only an accident saves his father from the same fate. That his wife and children, and not other persons, are the victims of his madness is the terrible but accidental result of their being at hand when the madness comes upon him. As the madness slowly passes off, he comes to understand what he has done. His friends believe that the madness was directly sent by Hera with the malignant purpose of making him murder his nearest and dearest. He too believes this at times; but there is at least one interval of complete sanity, during which he declares the gods incapable of crime and even of any sort of need. In the end his friend Theseus takes him away to make his home in Athens; but though Theseus thus makes a grateful return to the man who saved him 'from death under the earth', he does not say that he was saved from captivity in Hades, because neither of them had been in Hades.

This outline of the 'real story' of the play has already indicated, openly or by implication, those features of the ostensible story whose reality it denies. These features are, roughly speaking, those that may be called supernatural; those, in other words, that are not, and could not be, any part of the experience of a fifth-century Athenian. Fabulous monsters; the descent of living persons into Hades and their return therefrom; the existence, evil character, and intervention in human affairs, of the deities and sub-deities of the Olympian religion: none of these things, though we hear much of them, are *facts*. They cannot be facts; and they need not be facts. The real story is a coherent intelligible whole without them; it is also a moving and terrible picture of human suffering and disaster, and a deeply interesting study of human character; and the play itself, thus understood, is what it would not be otherwise, a good play, an artistic unity, satisfying both in its several parts and as a whole. This is, I hope, a not unfair summary of what Verrall believes about this play: let us now consider his reasons for believing it.[1]

He begins by calling our attention to six lines, spoken

---

[1] These reasons are discussed in the order in which they appear in Verrall's essay, for the convenience of those readers who have the essay before them.

by Heracles to Theseus, which are, from any point of view, of great importance. They are these (ll. 1341–6):

ἐγὼ δὲ τοὺς θεοὺς οὔτε λέκτρ' ἃ μὴ θέμις
στέργειν νομίζω, δεσμά τ' ἐξάπτειν χεροῖν
οὔτ' ἠξίωσα πώποτ' οὔτε πείσομαι,
οὔτ' ἄλλον ἄλλου δεσπότην πεφυκέναι.
δεῖται γὰρ ὁ θεός, εἴπερ ἐστ' ὀρθῶς[1] θεός,
οὐδενός· ἀοιδῶν οἵδε δύστηνοι λόγοι.

That is to say, the received traditions about the gods are false; a divine being cannot be guilty of immoral conduct due to the love of pleasure or power, for he is self-sufficient, in need of nothing, and therefore incapable of the desires that lead to such conduct in human beings. 'Nothing', says Verrall, 'could be plainer. The speaker rejects absolutely, and once for all, such man-like superhuman beings, such deities with the passions of men, as the common legend of Heracles...requires us to assume.' This is true; it is also true that the words cannot be explained as due to 'self-deception, delusion or pretence'. They express, too, without doubt, what Euripides himself believed; and they express his hostility to the received traditions, a hostility not to be appeased by the mild purgative treatment with which poets like Aeschylus or Pindar tried to purify the traditions and make them credible.

But Verrall now adds this: 'We must understand, and no one has ever attempted to prove the contrary, that it [this profession of faith] is given for the real opinion of the dramatic character presented, a part and an essential part of his mind.' I do not think that we 'must' understand this. The contrary, if it cannot actually be proved, may be shown to be far more likely; and if this can be shown, we can avoid Verrall's inference, which other-

[1] ὄντως, not ὀρθῶς, may be the true reading; but it matters little.

wise it would, I agree, be hard to avoid, that 'the legend of Heracles, as commonly told, is not to be supposed as part of the story, but replaced by some totally different conception of Heracles, and of his mental and physical history'. If such a replacement were indeed necessary, it would be hard to devise a new conception of the Heracles story more probable than Verrall's. Those who find Verrall's conception untenable are therefore bound to show, if they can, that neither it nor any other new conception is needed at all; and to do this they must take up Verrall's challenge, and show that the six lines before us are not 'the real opinion of the dramatic character presented, a part and an essential part of his mind'.

Before attempting this, let us consider two facts about the six lines: one concerns their content, the other their context.

(i) The last two lines, or at least the words δεῖται ὁ θεὸς οὐδενός, imply a far more radical assault upon received tradition than the first four lines imply. To the general spirit, if not to the details, of the first four lines many 'orthodox' persons—Aeschylus and Pindar, for instance—might well assent. The doctrine *here* expressed is consistent with the Olympian religion, purged of its grosser features; it requires us to reject as δύστηνοι some only of the ἀοιδῶν λόγοι, not all of them; it is consistent with all the facts in the received story of Heracles, except that of his being the son of Zeus by Alcmene. (It is perhaps consistent even with this; for the story of the play does not *compel* us to believe him the son of Zeus. That is indeed the only reason given for Hera's hating him, but other reasons are conceivable.) But the last two lines are a very different matter. The principle δεῖται ὁ θεὸς οὐδενός flatly contradicts the whole Olympian religious system, its theory and its practice alike, and implies that the ostensible course of events in this play is an impossible fiction. However, this distinction forms no objection to Verrall's view; for the last two lines colour the first four, not the first four the last two.

(ii) The six lines are, in the mouth of Heracles, an answer to words of Theseus (ll. 1314–21). Theseus finds Heracles crushed by his load of guilt, and reminds him that the gods often commit crimes, and nevertheless continue to 'bear up' pretty well: shall he, a mere man, set up for himself a higher standard than the divine one? To this Heracles replies that the argument is beside the mark,[1] for the gods do not commit crimes. The context of the six lines thus gives them a natural and definite place in the action of the play. Up to a point, they may even be felt to suit the character and circumstances of the speaker: so far, namely, as they convey the simple idea that he is an honest decent man, who has never thought of the gods as cheerful criminals, and is not able to excuse or comfort himself by so thinking of them now. But though the lines do mean this, they mean much more. They are a precise and emphatic statement of a far-reaching theological dogma; and in so far as they are this, we have still to ask what the purpose of Euripides is when he puts them into the mouth of Heracles.

The only possible alternative account of them is that, for the moment, Euripides has abandoned dramatic verisimilitude, and is making Heracles merely the mouthpiece of his own views. About such a proceeding we may ask several questions.

(i) Is it aesthetically justifiable, compatible with the opinion that Euripides is a great artist? The first

---

[1] 1340 πάρεργα τῶν ἐμῶν κακῶν, 'irrelevant to my woes'. So far as the immediate argument goes, this description is a little euphemistic. The argument is 'irrelevant' because, being based on a false premiss, it is essentially unsound.

judgement of a modern reader may be that it is not: that either Euripides has not done this, or, if he has, he has offended against a canon of literary art. But such judgements are a shaky basis for argument. The canons of art, literary or other, are not all immutable. This canon—that the *dramatis personae* of tragedy must always speak in character—is not so self-evident that we are bound to suppose it obeyed, consciously or subconsciously, by all good Greek poets. No one questions the fact that in more than one of his plays Euripides offers us, through the mouths of his characters, satirical attacks upon the dramatic technique of Aeschylus. Our first judgement of this fact, if we are honest, is probably that this, too, is bad art; and as we cannot doubt the fact itself, we condemn Euripides. Must we do the same in the matter before us, if we accept the fact itself here too? Or shall we rather—having reflected on the many important respects in which ancient Greek tragedy differs from modern drama—take it that not even the most sensitive Greek critic would find anything amiss in either of the two proceedings just mentioned? In that case our own aesthetic disapproval can be no argument against the alternative hypothesis we are now considering: Heracles may be speaking out of character, and Euripides be none the less a great artist.

(ii) This leads to a second question: Can the alleged proceeding be paralleled? Not much space need be taken to prove that it can. It is so common that Decharme devotes a paragraph to considering the criteria by which we may discern the utterances that are not in character, but simply convey Euripides' own opinions. More important, he shows that Lucian and Dionysius of Halicarnassus were familiar with Euripides' practice in this matter.[1] Rightly or wrongly in our eyes, with or

---

[1] *Euripides and the Spirit of his Dramas*, pp. 20-1.

without the approval even of his own age, he did such things often; and most of his readers would say, at first sight, that this is what he has done in the passage we are considering. If, as Verrall says, no one has ever attempted to prove this, the reason may be that no one has thought it needed proving.

(iii) It must, however, be admitted that, even if Euripides did such things often, he did not do them so often as to let us suppose that he did them lightly and casually; and the subjects on which he thus addresses his public would lead us to the same conclusion, being usually if not always matters of serious importance. If we now ask whether the subject of these six lines is one about which he was likely to feel strongly, the question almost answers itself. No one doubts altogether his hostility to the received religious traditions. The only differences of opinion concern the strength of that hostility, and the extent to which it affected him as poet and playwright. Other passages of the same character are numerous enough to show that on no topic was he more prone to abandon dramatic verisimilitude and make a *dramatis persona* his own mouthpiece. And since in no play do the received religious traditions present the gods in a more discreditable light than in the *Heracles*, it is likely that in this play he should do what he does elsewhere, and tell his public directly what his personal opinion of those traditions is. It may be added that this is the only passage in the play where, so far at least as this topic is concerned, dramatic verisimilitude is abandoned.

It may occur to the reader at this point that it matters very little, after all, whether in these six lines dramatic verisimilitude is abandoned or preserved. In either case, he may argue, Euripides here tells us that the received

66

story of Heracles, if for no other reason than that it depicts the gods as what the gods are not, is an incredible fiction. The received story is nevertheless ostensibly that of the play. Are we not bound, therefore, to seek to reinterpret the play, as Verrall would have us do, either on his own lines or (if we can think of them) on other lines, even if not for his reason? My own answer to this question is given by the general thesis of this book. If we suppose that Euripides in this play is presenting us with a series of events which, in his opinion, did occur or might have occurred, then, since he tells us plainly that what he *seems* to show us did not occur and could not have occurred, we shall be forced to attempt reinterpretation, to discover, if we can, what he is *really* showing us; and it will not be easy, as I have said, to better the reinterpretation made by Verrall. My thesis is that we need not suppose this; that Euripides says to us, in effect: 'What you see in my play could not have occurred; but if the received story were true, what *would* have occurred is just what you see in my play.'

But we are concerned, for the moment, not with those who are disposed to accept my thesis, but with those who are not, and in particular with those who think Verrall right, in the main if not in all details. And it is of course not enough to show that he was misled by his too hasty assumption that the six lines we have been considering express the real mind of Heracles. This assumption is the starting-point of his argument, and an important part of it; but it is by no means the whole of it. It is not, indeed, in itself any part of the actual reinterpretation of the play, but simply a provoking cause of that reinterpretation. A cause, not *the* cause; for there is another which Verrall states plainly. Taken at its face value, he thinks the play would be an extremely ill-executed piece of work, as

67   5-2

many others have thought and said that it is: that it would be the 'grotesque abortion' Swinburne said it was, 'a monster, a chaos, in which incommunicable parts are joined or mixed without disguise and without attempts at reconciliation'. Now if this were clearly true, it would indeed be a further reason why we, knowing the great reputation Euripides enjoyed throughout Greece, should not take this play at its face value, but do our best to reinterpret it. But it is not, to say the least of it, clearly true. In the first place, not all modern critics hold the violent opinion quoted; most of them, I think, would neither form such an opinion for themselves nor be persuaded into such an opinion by the arguments of others. And further, what is more important, even if such an opinion were general among us, it might well arise from a weakness to which the learned scholar, the subtle critic, the inspired poet, may be as subject as other people: I mean the inability to grasp, or at least to bear constantly in mind, certain radical differences between the ancient and the modern conception of what a stage-play should be, differences which affect profoundly the structure and arrangement, not less than the substantial content, of ancient and modern plays. Of this I speak in my last chapter. For the moment it is enough to insist that dissatisfaction with the structure of the *Heracles* should not be thought an overwhelmingly strong reason for trying to reinterpret the whole meaning of the play, since such dissatisfaction may be due to our making assumptions, about Greek tragedies in general, which we have no right to make.

I will now try to indicate what seem to me to be some of the weak points of the reconstruction that Verrall propounds, with his usual subtlety and eloquence, in his essay on the *Heracles*. He begins by saying what is quite true, that the rationalizing of myths, and not least of the Heracles myth, was by now a current practice; but he infers that the presentation of a tragedy based upon such a rationalized myth is no matter for surprise; and this inference cannot easily be justified, if we consider what tragedy in general had been and still was. Next he assumes, with little attempt at proof, that Euripides was curious to know how the more incredible myths gained credence, and that he was dissatisfied with the explanation of this process given by the common run of rationalizers: neither of these assumptions can be made safely. Then he argues that Euripides found the topic of mental aberration attractive, and that we have 'abundant evidence' from other plays that 'the imagination of insane and irregular minds' appeared to him a probable source of many incredible myths. It would take too long to examine here the 'abundant evidence' offered to us;[1] it does not seem to me convincing. At best it could only give some little support to the next assertion, that it is in the *Heracles* that we have the fullest and most impressive instance of myth as the offspring of madness. The madness of Heracles, we are told, does not begin with the arrival of Iris and Lyssa; he has long been subject to intermittent delusions, which both foster and are fostered by the delusions of other people (who are not, however, regarded as themselves insane), concerning his birth and his exploits. Under the influence of these delusions, much in himself and in his exploits that is wonderful indeed, but still human and natural, has been transformed, in his own mind and in the minds of others, into what is superhuman and supernatural. The knowledge of these delusions has preyed upon his mind in his saner hours; 'self-hatred and self-suspicion' have

[1] *Four Plays of Euripides*, p. 140, where references are given in footnotes.

increased 'the inner mischief from which they spring'; and the 'special excitement' caused by the events that follow his home-coming makes his brain give way completely. He becomes for a time a homicidal maniac, and unfortunately the victims of his mania are his wife and his children.

What are we to say of this picture? That it is, in itself, fanciful and unconvincing, in all its parts and as a whole? That it could not have been imagined, far less accepted, by a Greek of the fifth century B.C.? That if it could, it would not have been grasped by any appreciable number of his hearers or readers, even if it had been plainly set forth in a fashion in which it neither was nor could be set forth? All this, I believe, may fairly be said. Admittedly the picture is coherent; the psychology is something less than a stark impossibility; and if Heracles' madness is to be taken as due to 'natural causes' at all the causes must be these, or something like these. But unless what we find in the play itself gives very clear support to this startling theory, we must refuse to believe that the madness is in fact represented as due to natural causes, or in other words, that the myth has, in this respect at least, been rationalized. And what support for the theory are we offered from the play itself?

The evidence from the first part of it may be grouped roughly under three heads.

(i) First, we are told that Megara, Lycus and the Theban supporters of Lycus do not hold Heracles to be the son of Zeus, nor his deeds to be miraculous.—But that Megara does not is not proved. She does not say that she does, but neither does she say that she does not. She despairs of help from him, indeed; she believes him dead; but demigods, from Homer's time onwards, are mortal. And why, in any case, must she, and why must

Lycus and his friends, be right in their unbelief, any more than Amphitryon and the Chorus right in their belief?

(ii) But next, we are told that Amphitryon and the Chorus do not produce convincing evidence for their belief. Is it reasonable to expect this? Lycus has denied the heroic courage of Heracles: Amphitryon in his reply seeks to prove, not that Heracles really did this or that great deed, but that, having admittedly done them, he clearly possesses heroic courage. The business of the Chorus is not further proof, either of Heracles' deeds or of their bravery, but simple encomium, the dramatic value of which is surely as potent as its lyric beauty.

(iii) Thirdly, we are told what, if it could be maintained, would be a very strong rationalist argument, that Heracles himself, between his first arrival and his homicidal outburst, does not behave and speak like a wholly sane man. Some four reasons for thinking so are offered us. (*a*) He threatens instant death to Lycus and his friends, 'single-handed revenge upon a whole population'. (*b*) He finds time to salute his household gods, and to speak of his adventure in Hades, in spite of the pressing danger of his position. (*c*) The tone in which he speaks of his adventure in Hades is not that of a sane man reporting facts. (*d*) Amphitryon and Megara display uneasiness about both his physical safety and his mental stability.—These four sentences sum up, briefly but I hope fairly, the evidence for Heracles' incipient madness. They do not make up a strong case. (*a*) The threat of vengeance is natural for a great warrior strongly excited, and is not absurd unless we asume that he is not very much more formidable than anyone else, which would of course be to beg the whole question. (*b*) The danger is not so pressing that no moment may be lost; and if it were, why does Amphitryon, who does not (we are told) share his confidence, detain him in talk? But in any case such an argument, though it might have some force for a modern realistic play, has little or none for a Greek tragedy, in which the lapse of time required by the facts of the story has almost no relation to the time occupied in stage performance. (*c*) Of the tone of Heracles' tale the reader must judge for himself: I find no support in the text for Verrall's assertion. (*d*) Amphitryon and Megara may well be uneasy, on any hypothesis, about the hero's physical safety, which after all involves their own. But about his mental stability I see no sign in the text that they feel any uneasiness at all. Megara's silence after his 'vengeance' speech no more proves her thus uneasy than Amphitryon's silence,[1] from Heracles' first arrival till over sixty lines have been spoken by others, proves either uneasiness or anything else. It should be noted as a general principle that arguments from silence, like arguments from lapse of time, are never safe in Greek tragedy: we may argue from what *is* said or done, not—or only very tentatively indeed—from what is *not* said or done.

We come now to the appearance of Iris and Lyssa. The difficulty that their appearance in person causes the rationalist is obvious. Are they real, or are they not? Rationalism prevents our taking them as real; and once more Verrall insists that the six lines already discussed force rationalism upon us. But if Iris and Lyssa are not real, what are they? 'They are, they must be, a *vision*, the picture of someone's imagination, presented externally for theatrical convenience, but not supposed to have any reality other than that of the imagining mind.' Who,

---

[1] It is doubtful whether the last part of l. 531 should be assigned to him or to Megara.

then, see the vision? The Chorus. After their ode of triumph, they fall asleep, worn out; as they sleep, they dream, and their dream is what the spectators see with their eyes. What causes the dream? Their subconscious awareness, attained while they were still awake, that Heracles is already not sane. Consciously, they were at ease, confident, triumphant: subconsciously, they knew better. Consciousness passes into sleep, and the subconscious, as in all dreams, asserts itself. The vision is not, of course, a vision of truth. That would contradict the six lines as fully as a real Iris and a real Lyssa would contradict them. It is 'a theological nightmare', not a theological revelation. Such, in essence, is Verrall's solution of this difficulty. It is hard to think of a better one that would be consistent with the rationalized account of the play; yet the objections to this one are neither few nor trivial.

(i) The most serious, perhaps, is that no other instance can be quoted, from ancient drama, of the 'expressionist' technique by which actors represent unreal beings who are merely the product of real beings' imagination. 'The device is familiar enough', we are told; but the illustration given is not from ancient drama but from Shakespeare, and even so is not fully parallel, for Richard III's phantoms, if unreal, at least symbolize what is true, whereas Iris and Lyssa, or at any rate Iris, can symbolize only what is false. And if Euripides had indeed been the first 'expressionist' would he have introduced the device without one spoken word to help the astonished spectator to understand it?—especially seeing that—as Verrall himself rightly insists—Euripides wrote for readers as well as for spectators.

(ii) What parallel can be found, on the stage or elsewhere in the ancient world, for the subconscious formation and retention, not to speak of the subsequent expression, of an idea or emotion that is the exact contrary of what is simultaneously being thought or felt consciously? Is not the whole notion the product of modern psychical research?

(iii) Is the vision a dream, in the ordinary sense, or a waking hallucination? Verrall clearly makes it a dream: he supposes the Chorus to fall asleep from age and weariness after l. 814, and to be waked by the messenger at l. 910. Yet somehow they manage to speak, while thus asleep, not only about the imaginary creatures of their vision, but about the anguished cries of Amphitryon within the house, and about the earthquake[1] that makes Heracles, also within the house, cry out with terror. If they are asleep, how can they speak of these things, or even be aware of them?

(iv) Because the Chorus do not speak of their vision in the latter part of the play, Verrall argues that they must have forgotten it, and that they could not have forgotten it unless it had been a dream. Apart from the general weakness, already pointed out, of all 'arguments from silence', the first step of this particular argument is very weak. A dream is not always forgotten. The share of the Chorus in this latter part of the play is very small; but small as it is, they say several things that are most easily explained, to say the least of it, by taking them to remember their vision. ἄλαστα τὰν δόμοισι, cries the messenger at his first appearance, and the response of the Chorus is μάντιν οὐχ ἕτερον ἄξομαι: this surely means 'I know, I know: your words need no confirmation', not as Verrall takes it 'I foreboded some horrible thing' (l. 912). δάιοι δὲ τοκέων χέρες (l. 915), if spoken by the Chorus (as the MSS. assign them: Verrall naturally

---

[1] It is, I admit, uncertain by whom ll. 904-8 are spoken.

prefers not to do so), are words most simply taken as
expressing what is already known, not as a sudden
divination; and the same is true of πῶς παισὶ στενακτὰν
ἄταν ἄταν πατέρος ἀμφαίνεις; (ll. 917–18), which are
clearly words spoken by the Chorus.[1] Verrall himself
admits that in τίνα τρόπον ἔσυτο θεόθεν ἐπὶ μέλαθρα κακὰ
τάδε; 'we may perhaps see a faint trace of the vanished
vision' (ll. 919–20). In the lyric passage (ll. 1016–85) no
unprejudiced reader will feel the lack of any allusion to
Iris and Lyssa surprising. After that passage the Chorus
are almost silent to the end of the play; and yet, of their
four short utterances, two express convictions about the
source of Heracles' madness that may spring from
simple intuition, but are far more naturally attributable
to memory of the vision. Ll. 1086–7:

> ὦ Ζεῦ, τί παῖδ' ἤχθηρας ὧδ' ὑπερκότως
> τὸν σόν, κακῶν δὲ πέλαγος ἐς τόδ' ἤγαγες;

recall the statement of Iris that Zeus is now letting Hera
have her way (ll. 827–32); and ll. 1311–12 point to the
vision even more clearly:

> οὐκ ἔστιν ἄλλου δαιμόνων ἀγὼν ὅδε,
> ἢ τῆς Διὸς δάμαρτος· εὖ τόδ' αἰσθάνῃ.

Why should Heracles' words (ll. 1303–10) carry such
strong conviction to the Chorus—especially if, as
Verrall insists, Heracles is still far from being himself—
unless they are convinced on other grounds?

(v) Why do the Chorus dream just what they do?
Verrall admits that the question is a fair one; but what is
his answer? 'Their dreams are a disordered reflexion or
suggestion from their previous experience when awake.'
But let us consider what the actual dialogue between

---

[1] ἀμφαίνεις simply means 'tell the story of': the Chorus know the
main fact, but not the details; they ask for these now.

Iris and Lyssa implies. It implies that the action of Hera is that of a jealous, cruel, unjust being: that it is so wicked as to revolt the spirit of Madness herself. What previous experience can the pious and orthodox old men have had that could suggest such a dream to them? Have they been reading Xenophanes' poem, or heard Euripides himself candidly expressing his opinion of the Olympian gods? Nothing less seems an adequate cause for such an effect. And the more 'disordered' we suppose the 'reflexion or suggestion' to be, the more we label it a 'phantasmagoria' or 'nightmare', so much the more pointless and purposeless it becomes for the purpose of the play. And let us note this, that however psychologically natural such a dream might appear, it has no conceivable point or purpose in the drama. It would be otherwise if it conveyed to the dreamers, and through them to the spectators, something that was in some sense and in some degree true. But *ex hypothesi* it does not. We have therefore to repeat our question, 'Why do the Chorus dream just what they do?' in a new sense. We now ask not how the psychology of the dream can be justified, but what motive can have caused Euripides to put in the scene at all. A nightmare, false and misleading in itself, and forgotten as soon as it is over, so that its occurrence cannot and does not affect either the actions or the thoughts either of the Chorus or of anyone else— what is it, what can it be for? To *this* question I cannot see that Verrall attempts an answer, or that, deeply and rightly concerned as he always is to defend Euripides as an artist, he had even considered the difficulty at all.

There is one detail in the messenger's terrible tale of madness and murder that Verrall notices, indeed, but leaves without any real attempt at explanation, though it is not unimportant for his case that it should be explained. I refer to the incident of the stunning of Heracles as he is about to kill Amphitryon. The messenger's tale attributes this, briefly but clearly, to Athena. She strikes Heracles on the breast with a stone (ll. 1001–9):

> ἔρριψε πέτρον στέρνον εἰς Ἡρακλέους
> ὅς νιν φόνου μαργῶντος ἔσχε, κεἰς ὕπνον
> καθῆκε· πίτνει δ' ἐς πέδον....

This incident is closely connected, if not precisely identical, with what we are made aware of in ll. 904–9, just before the messenger enters. There the following words appear in the text:

> ἰδοὺ ἰδού,
> θύελλα σείει δῶμα, συμπίτνει στέγη.
> —ἤ ἤ· τί δρᾷς, ὦ Διὸς παῖ, μελάθρῳ;
> τάραγμα ταρτάρειον, ὡς ἐπ' Ἐγκελάδῳ ποτέ, Παλλάς,
>   ἐς δόμους πέμπεις.

We cannot be sure to whom these words should be assigned: any, or all, may be uttered by the Chorus, or by Heracles within, or by Amphitryon within. The house is shaken by a violent wind, and some part of it, at least, collapses; and Athena is seen by someone causing this to happen. This the words clearly convey: this, and nothing more. Comparing the passage with the messenger's report quoted above, we must suppose either that Athena shakes the house so that a falling stone strikes Heracles, or that she first shakes the house and then picks up a fallen stone and throws it at Heracles. Now what Verrall should have told us, but has not, is what really happens here. The agency of Athena being excluded, what shakes the house, and what strikes Heracles down? Is there an earthquake or hurricane— by a chance coincidence? Or does Heracles himself knock down part of the house? Verrall merely speaks

77

of Amphitryon's being saved 'by a chance blow, received by the madman from the falling ruins of the chamber, which he, by a turn in his delusion, interprets fortunately'. This implies what is certainly possible, that Heracles is the speaker of the words

τί δρᾷς, ὦ Διὸς παῖ, μελάθρῳ;

and those that follow, and that his belief in Athena's being the cause of the shaking is a new delusion. But this does not tell us what Verrall takes to be the real cause of the shaking, why the new delusion is fortunate,[1] or how the messenger comes to share that delusion. I can see no answer to these questions that will square at once with the facts of the text and with a rationalized version of the story.

With Verrall's handling of the last part of the play I shall deal briefly, because, if my criticism of his handling of the earlier part is sound, and my interpretation of the six lines (1341–6) correct, the last part of the play presents no serious difficulties. Except for the six lines, all the supernatural features of the Heracles story, including those in what has just happened, are taken for granted by all the persons on the stage, from the moment at which Heracles recovers consciousness to the close of the play. Verrall is, indeed, far from admitting this. In particular he maintains that Theseus never says anything that shows any belief in these supernatural features, or anything that in any other way furnishes any clear evidence for them. This, as it happens, is true, or all but true. But it is a weak argument. For there is almost no occasion for any reference to these topics by Theseus. What references he does make to them at least point to

---

[1] As to this, can Verrall mean that the messenger's words ὃς νιν φόνου μαργῶντος ἔσχε refer to a *mental* change in Heracles? The madman, surely, is suddenly stunned: ἔσχε means 'stopped', not 'dissuaded'.

belief rather than to disbelief. Take the topic of which Verrall makes much, the adventure in Hades. When Theseus speaks of his deliverance from Hades by Heracles, and uses such expressions as σώσας με νέρθεν and ὅτ᾽ ἐξέσωσάς μ᾽ ἐς φάος νεκρῶν πάρα, it is indeed possible to make these words fit an escape from entombment in a cavern or mine containing a number of dead men. But it is not too much to call this an arbitrary and crazy distortion of what the words would convey to any ancient spectator or reader. If the adventure in Hades was real, why, Verrall asks, does Theseus not speak of it in language that cannot be misunderstood? We may reply by asking why Theseus does not speak in such language if the adventure was *not* real. That is what the spectator and reader would need—something that shall exclude the supernatural definitely, not something that merely fails to confirm it. Verrall speaks almost as if the central topic of this last scene of the play were the truth or falsity of the divine birth and miraculous deeds of Heracles; almost as if Theseus' main purpose should not have been to comfort and save his best friend from despair and suicide, but to defend against incredulous scoffers his reputation as son of Zeus and doer of super-human marvels.

Of course the whole interest and meaning of this noble concluding scene is utterly different from this. It is indeed a good instance, perhaps the best, of how real and therefore how moving a picture Euripides can draw of human character, human relations and human destiny, in spite of its being blended with a quite different picture, a satirical, a ludicrous, repulsive and incredible picture of the gods and their dealings with men. And of course Verrall knew this, and felt this, as fully and finely as the best among us can ever hope to do; and here as elsewhere, his fantastic ingenuities are due to no lack of subtlety or candour or common sense; they are the unhappy if inevitable outcome of the rationalist hypothesis, that brilliant hypothesis which may be said to have every merit except that of conformity with the facts.

This chapter has up to this point been concerned solely with the attempt to show that Verrall's interpretation of the *Heracles* is untenable. It does not of course follow, even from the fullest acceptance of my arguments and conclusion, that his interpretation of other plays is equally unsound, or unsound at all; and for this reason among others, that the thesis he seeks to defend is some-times—notably in the case of the *Andromache*—of a very different nature from his thesis regarding the *Heracles*. Nevertheless, I must be content with discussing his treatment of this one play. A full discussion of all the others would be found tedious by those who are not disposed to agree with him: anything less would be unfair to him and would fail to convince his supporters. What has already been said will perhaps be enough to make some at least of his supporters ready to consider an alternative theory which owes much to him, fully accepts a most important part of his own theory, and invites for that part the recognition hitherto withheld from it by critics who perceive the weakness of the rest. I now ask for the attention of all my readers alike while I try to apply this alternative theory of mine to the *Heracles*, in the hope that their consideration of Verrall's view of the play will have prepared the way for a judgement of my own view of it.

I hold, then, that this play, like many others, and as much as any others, is to be looked upon as what I have called, for want of a better name, a *fantasy*: that is, an inseparable complex of the credible and the incredible which because of the incredible part of it is incredible as a whole. All that we see, and all that we hear, is to be taken at its face value. The divine beings are to be considered no less real than the human beings, and as causing the effects which the human beings attribute to them. Heracles is to be taken as quite sane until the moment when Lyssa begins to madden him, and as quite sane from the moment of his recovering consciousness. His adventures, including the journey to Hades, have in fact been just what he and others believe and say they have been; and well they may be, for he is no ordinary man, but the son of Zeus himself. And so on, for all the details of the myth and of the play, except for the famous six lines, which are in effect not part of the play at all, but a comment upon it by the poet himself.

To take the play thus at its face value is the attitude of nearly all modern readers of it. But unless we are to abandon this attitude, we cannot leave the matter there. There is no play of Euripides regarding which we may feel more certain that he did not believe it, and could not have believed it, to represent a series of events which did happen or could have happened; that he found some of these events intellectually incredible, or morally repulsive, or both. The six lines are by themselves enough to prove this true. Whether they do or do not express the real mind of the Heracles of the play, beyond question they express the real mind of Euripides; and I am not aware that anyone has denied or doubted this. There are many other things in the play that point in the same direction, some of which have attracted attention, though I think not all. No one of them is, so to put it, external to the play, in the sense in which this may be said of the six lines; and the cumulative effect of all of them would not, if the six lines were wanting, prove what the six lines by themselves are enough to prove. But taken in conjunction with the six lines, they should leave us in less doubt than ever. Let us look at the more important of them.

(i) Amphitryon, despairing of deliverance from Lycus through the intervention of Zeus, reproaches Zeus in these words (ll. 339–47):

> ὦ Ζεῦ, μάτην ἄρ' ὁμόγαμόν σ' ἐκτησάμην,
> μάτην δὲ παιδὸς κοινεῶν' ἐκλῄζομεν·
> σὺ δ' ἦσθ' ἄρ' ἧσσον ἢ 'δόκεις εἶναι φίλος.
> ἀρετῇ σε νικῶ θνητὸς ὢν θεὸν μέγαν·
> παῖδας γὰρ οὐ προύδωκα τοὺς Ἡρακλέους·
> σὺ δ' ἐς μὲν εὐνὰς κρύφιος ἠπίστω μολεῖν,
> τἀλλότρια λέκτρα δόντος οὐδενὸς λαβών,
> σῴζειν δὲ τοὺς σοὺς οὐκ ἐπίστασαι φίλους.
> ἀμαθής τις εἶ θεός, ἢ δίκαιος οὐκ ἔφυς.

To call these words blasphemous would be unjust, even from the most orthodox point of view: not only because they seem justified by the facts; not only because, even if unjustified, they are the natural and excusable outcome of despair; but also because orthodoxy did not in fact mean any effective belief that even Zeus himself is perfectly wise and just. To Euripides the words must have seemed an entirely fair comment on the supposed facts, and the final dilemma unescapable. They conveyed a sound argument leading to an incredible conclusion, the conclusion that the supreme deity must be either a fool or a knave. Therefore the premises are false; the supposed facts are not facts but fictions.

(ii) Critics do not, for the most part, think very well of the first third of the play, or indeed of the first half of it. They do not agree about the purpose of this long tale of peril followed by deliverance, and none of the purposes suggested seem adequate even to those who suggest them. They do agree that, whatever this purpose was, this tale lasts too long, and that it has no organic relation, or at least not enough, with what comes after it. These constructive defects are not atoned for by any great interest in the character-drawing. Lycus is particularly uninteresting, says Wilamowitz-Moellendorff.[1] He is 'nothing but a conventional stage villain', without morals or intelligence or even manners, whose appeal could only be to the less sophisticated part of the audience.[2] Such strictures, if not quite unjustified, seem excessive. The story is not two stories loosely joined. The fortunes of Heracles are so closely linked with the fortunes of his family that the first reversal of them is almost as much as the second the reversal of his own: the play is about Heracles from the outset. And the character and behaviour of Lycus have a significance that has perhaps escaped notice. We are, and are meant to be, indifferent to his fate. He is a scoundrel, and deserves his doom. But he is less of a scoundrel than Zeus and Hera. He has at least the motive of self-preservation to justify his cruelty, whereas Hera's motive is sheer malignity, and for the acquiescence of Zeus no motive at all is suggested. There is even something like courtesy in the manner of Lycus when he puts forward this motive of his as his defence (ll. 165–9):

> ἔχει δὲ τοὐμὸν οὐκ ἀναίδειαν, γέρον,
> ἀλλ' εὐλάβειαν· οἶδα γὰρ κατακτανὼν
> Κρέοντα πατέρα τῆσδε καὶ θρόνους ἔχων.
> οὔκουν τραφέντων τῶνδε τιμωροὺς ἐμοὺς
> χρῄζω λιπέσθαι τῶν δεδραμένων δίκην.

Unless Plato misleads us badly when he makes Polus

[1] See his edition of the play, I, 118.
[2] 'Ein naives Publikum wird an dieser Figur und ihrer Bestrafung seine Freude haben; damit hat Euripides aber nur für das Parterre, zum Teil nur für die Gallerie gearbeitet.'

6-2

tell Socrates that everyone, Socrates included, would, if
he could, copy the example of Archelaus and wade
through slaughter to a throne,[1] the conduct of Lycus,
while of course not admirable, would seem at least
defensible; and Euripides had to make him as nearly
complete a villain as he has ever depicted in order to
avoid the obvious artistic fault of making his fate seem
tragic. But for the divine persecutors of Heracles
nothing can be said and nothing is said. Lycus, again,
is sensitive enough to the claims of both religion and
decency to grant, readily, and without contempt or
insult, Megara's petition to be given time to array his
victims in their grave-clothes (ll. 327–35): the victims
of the Olympian gods are struck down as they are
gathered in festal attire, offering solemn sacrifice and
thanksgiving to the Olympian gods themselves; and
finally, a horror even more hideous, if possible, to the
Greeks than to us, their actual slayer is not a stranger
like Lycus, but their father, husband and son.[2] These
gods are viler even than the vile Lycus; and as the
parallelism implies that they are no less literally and
concretely real than Lycus himself, we hardly need the
six lines later to assure us of Euripides' purpose and
meaning: the tale he presents is not possible fact, but
fiction.

(iii) The triumph-song of the Chorus (ll. 735–814)
that accompanies and follows the slaying of Lycus
contains several passages worth our present attention:

(a)   τίς ὁ θεοὺς ἀνομίᾳ χραίνων, θνητὸς ὤν,
              ἄφρονα λόγον
          οὐρανίων μακάρων κατέβαλ', ὡς ἄρ' οὐ
              σθένουσιν θεοί;   (ll. 757–9.)

[1] *Gorgias*, 471 C–D.
[2] It is plainly against Hera's intention that Athena intervenes to save
Amphitryon.

84

(b)   θεοὶ θεοὶ
       τῶν ἀδίκων μέλουσι καὶ
       τῶν ὁσίων ἐπᾴειν.   (ll. 772–4.)

(c)   ὢ λέκτρων δύο συγγενεῖς
       εὐναί, θνατογενοῦς τε καὶ
       Διός, ὃς ἦλθεν ἐς εὐνὰν
       νύμφας τᾶς Περσηΐδος· ὡς
       πιστόν μοι τὸ παλαιὸν ἤδη
       λέχος, ὢ Ζεῦ, σὸν ἐπ' οὐκ ἐλπίδι φάνθη.
                                                   (ll. 798–804.)

The ode as a whole is, in view of the immediate sequel,
a clear and effective piece of dramatic irony. In that
quality the above passages share fully. But these are
something else as well; they are pieces of religious satire.
The second of the three needs little comment: we soon
see how much the gods care for righteousness and the
righteous man. The satire of the third passage bites
deep. The Chorus are convinced that Heracles is indeed
the son of Zeus, because Zeus has come to his aid and
given him victory: the sequel will not overthrow this
conviction as it will and must overthrow their faith in
divine justice; it will confirm this conviction, for that
Heracles is the son of Zeus is the only explanation of
Hera's cruelty. The first passage is remarkable for a
further reason. The Chorus exult in the discomfiture of
the impious and foolish blasphemer who has denied,
not the gods' wisdom, not their justice, but their *power*:
ὡς ἄρ' οὐ σθένουσιν θεοί. Here again we have an article of
faith which the sequel will not overthrow, but confirm
only too surely. But let us note what its rejection implies.
To deny the gods' wisdom and justice is compatible with
traditional orthodoxy, whatever Pindar and Aeschylus
may think: to deny the gods' power amounts to denying
their existence, to atheism. In the popular view there

could be little difference between simple atheism and the theism of Xenophanes, of Anaxagoras—and of Euripides. In these words Euripides supplies his orthodox opponents with a cap that seems designed to fit him exactly. It is hard to think that he has not done so intentionally. We need not, to be sure, class the passage with the six lines as extra-dramatic. Even if we allow the Chorus the full reality of a *dramatis persona*, a reality that it seldom possesses, we may still consider these words as 'in character'; there is no anachronism in supposing the existence of atheists in the days of Heracles. Yet nothing atheistic, no denial of the gods' power, has so far been uttered, or hinted at, in the course of the play: nothing, therefore, to which these words can be a specific allusion. The word σθένουσιν is consequently a little startling; and this is what it is probably meant to be. 'You call me blasphemer', says the poet to his audience and readers, 'for denying the gods' power: is it not worse blasphemy to assert that the gods, possessing power, use it as you believe they used it against Heracles?' But to present this play as embodying actual or possible fact would have been to assert exactly this.

(iv) In the scene between Iris and Lyssa, the element of religious satire is unmistakable, and it is needless to dilate upon its details. The most pungent of these is the revolt of the Spirit of Madness herself against the foul deed she is commanded to do. It stresses effectively the wickedness of Hera, both in its clear statement of facts (ll. 849–53) and by being the revolt, not of fallible man against the gods, but of one divine being against another. Polytheism, whether intellectually credible or not, is not in itself morally objectionable; but to the traditional polytheism of Greece, an essential feature of which was belief in discord and strife among the gods, the moral objections are strong, and to Euripides seem insuperable. It must indeed be allowed that this revolt of Lyssa's is exposed, as religious satire, to a criticism which it is hard to meet: namely, that it is the poet's own invention, not a part of the received tradition; we do not of course know this certainly, but it is altogether probable. The same is true of the callousness and absurd self-importance of Iris. The satirist can assail effectively what he finds already existing as tradition, and even what he can fairly and logically deduce therefrom: to knock down the Aunt Sally he has himself set up may be amusing, but helps his general purpose little. However, we are not now concerned to ask how far Euripides succeeded, or deserved to succeed, in this purpose of his, but only what his purpose was; and we can be sure that he did not mean to present the scene between Iris and Lyssa as what could in any sense be taken as true or possible.

(v) Athena's intervention to save Amphitryon's life is the one beneficent deed performed by a divine being. Euripides may have invented it—or, if it was part of the received tradition, adopted it—to please patriotic Athenians. But the compliment, if it is one, is not extravagant. Did she approve of the slaughter of the mother and children? Then she is little better than Zeus, Hera and Iris. Did she disapprove? Then why did she not come, or act, in time to save the mother and children too? Her late intervention classes her with the Dioscuri in the *Electra* (ll. 1298–1302) and Artemis in the *Hippolytus* (ll. 1325–34), whose excuses for their failure to avert the disasters they deplore are among the poet's most openly satirical utterances. Or was she perhaps merely acting as her father's agent, and has he, repenting at the last moment of having allowed Hera a completely free hand, dispatched his daughter to thwart this much

87

at least of his wife's purpose? In any case we cannot take Athena seriously. We are not, indeed, to rationalize her into an illusion of Heracles: she remains a necessary part of the story—and the story is fiction.

(vi) That Hera, with the sanction of Zeus, is the prime source of the fearful things that have come to pass—this is recognized not only by the Chorus, who saw and heard Iris and Lyssa, but by Amphitryon and Theseus and Heracles himself, who did not. This is but natural: they all know that Hera has been the implacable enemy of Heracles ever since he was born; this final horror, which it occurs to no one for a moment to suppose due to 'natural causes', is put down as a matter of course to the goddess who has always been his unrelenting persecutor. So much a matter of course, indeed, that we hear little recrimination: none save from Heracles, and from him one bitter outburst only (ll. 1303–10):

> χορευέτω δὴ Ζηνὸς ἡ κλεινὴ δάμαρ
> κρούουσ' Ὀλύμπου δῖον ἀρβύλῃ πέδον.[1]
> ἔπραξε γὰρ βούλησιν ἣν ἐβούλετο,
> ἄνδρ' Ἑλλάδος τὸν πρῶτον αὐτοῖσιν βάθροις
> ἄνω κάτω στρέψασα. τοιαύτῃ θεῷ
> τίς ἂν προσεύχοιθ'; ἢ γυναικὸς οὕνεκα
> λέκτρων φθονοῦσα Ζηνὶ τοὺς εὐεργέτας
> Ἑλλάδος ἀπώλεσ' οὐδὲν ὄντας αἰτίους.

Here, and here alone, that dignified reserve is abandoned that helps to set the heroic man high above the petty, treacherous, malignant gods. And even here the words are the words of a strong man and a sane man; and not one of them but is simple truth. It should be needless to point out that when Heracles cries, 'Who can pray to a goddess such as that?', he does not in the least question her existence. To suppose that is to make sheer nonsense

[1] The reading in l. 1304 is very doubtful; but the doubt cannot affect the general sense of the passage.

of the words that precede and follow.[1] His attitude is, 'She is there, she is mighty, but none the less she deserves no reverence or worship.'[2] This is the difference between Euripides and his Heracles: the attitude of Euripides is, 'She deserves no reverence or worship, and therefore not only is she not mighty, but she is not there at all'; and when we reach the six lines, this, in effect, is what is said. Thus, once more, we know what to think of our play. It is only too possible that men should believe in such deities as Hera: it is utterly impossible that such deities should exist.

(vii) Lastly, let us look again at Theseus' well-meant attempt to lighten Heracles' crushing sense of guilt, by arguing that the gods themselves, 'if the poets' tales are not false', have had their 'misfortunes', but nevertheless do not exile themselves from Olympus or give way to shame and despair (ll. 1314–21). What is the moral for Heracles?

καίτοι τί φήσεις, εἰ σὺ μὲν θνητὸς γεγὼς
φέρεις ὑπέρφευ τὰς τύχας, θεοὶ δὲ μή;

It is needless, unreasonable, even presumptuous, for him, a mortal man, to set up for himself a moral standard more exalted than that which satisfies the gods. Theseus does not mean—let us be clear about this—that Heracles is not a guilty sinner. Though he was the helpless instrument of a divine power, though in his heaven-sent madness he did not so much as know what he was doing, yet it is he, he and no other, who has done this awful

[1] Verrall, recognizing this, makes the cry arise from a sudden rush of sanity (see *Four Plays of Euripides*, pp. 189–90) after the madness of what precedes. But it must, I fear, be said that he makes this view seem plausible by mistranslating the last three and a half lines.
[2] Even in less exceptional circumstances a Greek could pick and choose among his deities. So Hippolytus pays special court to Artemis, but keeps Aphrodite 'at a distance' (*Hippolytus*, l. 102), without supposing Aphrodite less real or powerful than Artemis.

thing; his deed was not 'accidental homicide', but murder, and murder of the most hideous kind. No more than Oedipus may he try to rid himself of the sense of moral pollution by thinking of how and why the thing came to pass. This feeling, hardly comprehensible for us today, was universal in ancient Greece; it was shared even by Plato and Aristotle; there is no reason to think it was not shared by Euripides himself. And besides, the crimes imputed to the gods are not in any sense involuntary. No, Theseus' meaning is something simpler. Sin is sin, and horrible enough; but having committed it, we are to face the fact boldly. What is done cannot be undone, the sin as little as its consequences for its victims: technical purification ('there will I cleanse thy hands from pollution', l. 1324) is like exile from the scene of the sin, τοῦ νόμου χάριν. But this thought is consoling as well as terrible. The sinner's right course is to make the best of his life henceforward, not to yield weakly to the useless misery of remorse. Such is the counsel of Theseus to his friend; and such, in effect, is the course on which the stricken man in the end resolves. Such, we may even say, would be the right course even for the gods—if they could ever have sinned. It is their sinning, not their 'bearing up' nevertheless, that 'Heracles' in the six lines will not think possible. It is this false and impious premiss that makes the argument of Theseus fallacious, though the conclusion, taken as an independent proposition, is true, and good counsel. And further, this fallacious argument can be used, and was used,[1] for a far worse end than to dispel remorse; namely, to encourage sin: what gods have done men

---

[1] Cf. *Clouds*, 904. The argument seems to have been known in the Middle Ages, with scriptural heroes in place of Olympian gods (Froude, *Short Studies*, vol. IV (1894 ed.), pp. 16 and 55).

may do. That was a sound reason why anyone who took seriously his recognized duty of 'making his fellow-citizens better' should attempt to discredit the traditions that made such an argument plausible: as sound a reason as hatred of falsehood for its own sake. We cannot tell how far it weighed with Euripides: the present passage suggests, at least, that it weighed with him heavily. As the six lines, which soon follow, tell us clearly what he believed about the gods, so do these eight lines tell us, if less clearly, one reason why he would not keep his belief to himself, but wrote no play, if we may judge by those that have survived, that had not in it at least some touch of religious satire. No more need be said to show that this passage is evidence, less direct evidence than the others, but not less cogent, that Euripides meant this play to be taken, by sensible people, not as fact but as fiction; and not this play only, but all others where similar impious and immoral traditions about the gods are, despite their impiety and immorality, an integral part of the plot.

CHAPTER IV

THE *SUPPLIANTS* RECONSIDERED

[NOTE. Since the first paragraph (and indeed the whole of this chapter) was written, Professor Kitto's book on Greek Tragedy was published; and I may now claim his support for much that I have written here, though I go further than he does, and am not always in complete agreement with him.]

This chapter, like the one before it, will be devoted to the consideration of a single tragedy. The *Suppliants*, if my view of its tone and purpose is correct, has been more generally misunderstood, in certain respects, than any other play of Euripides. A right understanding of it, obviously desirable in any case on general grounds, will also be found to have a real though somewhat indirect bearing on the problem handled in the preceding chapters. For the moment, however, that problem, and the solution of it which I have propounded, may pass into the background, to be brought forward again in due course. Meanwhile it will be convenient at times, for my present purpose, to recall some facts already stated, and to repeat some arguments already advanced. Let us remind ourselves of one such thing forthwith: that all three solutions of our special problem—the rationalists', the symbolists', and my own—are alike in one respect, namely, in holding that Euripides wishes some of his readers, in some sense and to some extent, to perceive that he says one thing and means another. But however true this may be of some of the plays, and perhaps of most of them, it may not be true of all of them; and no critic seems to have suspected that it is true of the *Suppliants*.[1] The present chapter offers reasons for believing that the *Suppliants* is very far from being an exception to the general rule; very far from meaning just what at first sight it seems to mean.

The usual view of it may be more or less summed up in the final sentence of the small surviving fragment of the *hypothesis*: 'the play is an eulogy of the Athenians', τὸ δὲ δρᾶμα ἐγκώμιον 'Αθηναίων. By 'the Athenians' the writer of these words meant, we may safely suppose, not only the Athenians of the play, Theseus and his subjects, but also, and perhaps mainly, the Athenians of Euripides' own time, those for whom, and in whose presence, the play was performed. Not only is this the most natural meaning of the words themselves, but the greater part of what is said in the play about Athens and her citizens applies (conformably with Euripides' usual practice) much better to contemporary conditions than to those of the distant past. Understood thus, the dictum expresses fairly enough one thing, among others, which the play either in fact is or at least appears to be. The usual view is that it is in fact this: reasons will shortly be given for thinking otherwise. But it will clear the way to note that, whether it is this or not, there are two other things which (as will be agreed) it certainly is.

(i) It is a *play*, with a definite plot and action; a *tragedy*, a moving and beautiful picture of human misfortune and sorrow which are caused, not by great wickedness, but at worst by 'a mistake'—perhaps, in this case, by more than one mistake. It is this on the surface, and under the surface, and down to depths of

---

[1] Except Verrall; and he has not told us what he makes of this play; he has merely named it in passing as one of several whose face value is not their true value. And I must add Professor Kitto (see note prefixed to this chapter).

imaginative power of which few poets but Euripides have been capable, and which few of his readers would claim to fathom. If I do not deal, except incidentally, with the play as a work of imaginative art, let me not for that reason be supposed indifferent to its greatness and significance as such.

(ii) But further—and this is a fact highly relevant to our present inquiry—the play has a political purpose of a more particular kind than the stimulation of Athenian pride and patriotism by a general encomium. In March 420 Argos proposed an alliance between herself, Elis, Mantinea and Athens; and in July this alliance was concluded. It was supported by Alcibiades and Hyperbolus, opposed by Nicias. In form it was defensive; but the aim of at least some of its advocates was to renew the war with Sparta, and this may have been quite openly urged and clearly understood. The alliance was in any case a counter-move to the formal alliance made in the same month of March between Sparta and Boeotia. This move must have rekindled the exceptionally fierce resentment of Athens against Thebes that had been excited by the refusal of the Thebans, after the battle of Delium in 424, to surrender the Athenian dead for burial, a resentment which the Peace of Nicias had done little to allay. We need only consider the main events in the action of the *Suppliants* to see their relevance to the events of these years. Thebes refuses to surrender the Argive dead for burial; Athens gives active military help to Argos against Thebes; the play ends with the conclusion of a formal alliance between Argos and Athens, and the prediction of another invasion of Thebes by Argos. There is nothing else that tells us when the play was performed: but the facts just mentioned strongly suggest the year 420, and even the Great Dionysia in the

94

critical March of that year. In any case, the poet shows clear signs of wishing to influence public opinion about the Argive alliance. Ostensibly he supports the alliance: it is less certain that he means to be understood as doing so. We will come back to that question later. For the moment, my point is that the political position has not merely suggested to Euripides the choice of this particular subject out of the many available, but also, in accordance with the recognized right and duty of dramatic poets to *teach* their fellow-citizens, has induced him to urge upon them a particular line of action with regard to the great issues before them.

Still, the play may be both of these things, and yet 'eulogy of the Athenians' may be a fair enough description of its general spirit. The satirist, the critic, the reformer in Euripides may for once be taking a holiday. His feelings, his point of view, his purposes may for once be those of the majority of his countrymen. A harmony so unusual may be thought unlikely; but it is clearly not impossible. If it is actual fact, it follows that, whatever may be true of other plays, here at least there is no special appeal to the more discerning section of the audience. Here at least, such persons are not to be entertained by perceiving the author's tongue in his cheek. Here at least, they are to take him as meaning just what he must be taken to mean by the simple-minded and conventional and orthodox: just this, and nothing else as well as this or instead of this. It is this view of the *Suppliants*— hitherto, if I am not mistaken, almost universally accepted—which I examine in this chapter, having convinced myself that there are good grounds for rejecting it.

It may clear the issue if we note that in the *Suppliants* there is, in any case, no need and no room for 'rationalizing' the story: that is, for explaining away the supernatural and miraculous by suggesting that the story can and should be understood in a way that does not violate the uniformity of natural law, or conflict with what our experience tells us does or does not happen. For here the supernatural element, though not entirely lacking, is both very small and also not essential to the coherence of the play as a whole. Athena, to be sure, appears *ex machina* at the close; and what she says is, from another point of view, of great importance, as we shall see. But the story is, quite clearly, completed before she arrives: her part is purely that of an epilogue, which cannot certainly be said of all Euripides' theophanies. The success of the Athenians in battle with the Thebans is indeed attributed, by persons in the play, to divine support. But the most pious of Athenian spectators is given no special reason to attribute the success to divine support rather than to good luck, or to superiority in courage, efficiency or even numbers. The engulfing of Amphiaraus with his chariot is spoken of as a miracle wrought by Zeus. But this traditional incident is so unimportant that the most sceptical of Athenian spectators would give no more than a passing thought to what Euripides meant him to make of it. These three instances of the supernatural can be 'rationalized' easily enough by the followers of Verrall. Anyone willing to accept my 'fantasy' solution of a problem which in other plays is undoubtedly serious will accept it here as solving the very slight difficulties here presented: he will suppose that even here, though to a very slight extent, the story is not a presentation of actual or possible fact. Or again it is conceivable that Euripides is here taking a holiday from his usual sceptical criticism of the miracles of tradition; though we shall find reasons for doubting this. In any case, the difficulty arising from the super-natural element in this play is relatively slight, and needs no special attention.

The problem of the *Suppliants* is rather this. On the surface at any rate, the poet does not here attack, but supports, the political, social, moral and religious views of the majority of his countrymen. His treatment of the story of Theseus' rescue for burial, from the victorious Thebans, of the remains of the fallen Argives is made— is, on any showing, quite clearly made—the vehicle of a great many references to and comments on contem-porary Athens and her circumstances and problems; of which matters the Argive alliance is perhaps the most important, but is only one among many. In these references and comments, and in the attitude implied by much that is not explicit, it is quite clear that the poet wishes to show himself to his audience, or at any rate to some part of it, as a man who endorses heartily the popular traditions, and who supports certain active measures that correspond to those traditions. Is this the final truth of the matter? Or has Euripides even here a special message for the intelligentsia? Is the satirist and critic still very much alive in him, and by no means taking a holiday from duty? Much in the play suggests that this latter view is the true one.

Let us look more closely at the ostensible attitude adopted. The play represents Athens as the noble cham-pion of stricken Argos. With no ulterior motive, she makes war against Thebes, in defence of the unfortunate and oppressed, to maintain the law of Hellas and of the gods of Hellas. Her success in the struggle is no more than the due reward of her unselfish heroism. Theseus is a ruler worthy of such a people. He is devoutly religious, a brave warrior, a dutiful son: no τύραννος, but the unassuming βασιλεύς of a free democracy: if his will is law with his fellow-Athenians, it is not because they fear him, but because they love and trust him. There is no girding at orthodox religion or its gods, nothing that would seem to expose the poet to the charge of impiety. On the contrary, it is impiety that is said to have overthrown the Seven and their Argive army, and impiety that in the course of the play overthrows the Thebans. The mother of Theseus places duty to God in the forefront of her appeal to her son: duty to God is the final reason he himself gives for declaring war on Thebes. The right of the fallen to burial is not only a Πανελλήνων νόμος but a νόμος παλαιὸς δαιμόνων. Human valour avails nothing without divine support. The policy of Athens will be the right one only while Athena inspires it, her fortunes will be safe only while Athena defends her. Divination is one of the great blessings bestowed by the gods on mankind; and he is but a fool, or worse, who neglects or defies the diviners' predictions, as Adrastus did. There is no girding at democracy. The assault upon it is put into the mouth of the enemy's herald; the defence of it is made by the hero-king himself, and follows the strictest traditional lines. There is no girding at the spirit of militarism. Athens has grown famous and prosperous by it. The war of Athens against Thebes is fully justified by its purpose. The sons of the fallen Argive chieftains are solemnly enjoined by Athena herself to invade Thebes and take a bloody revenge on her as soon as they are old enough to do so.

Such are the ideas which, explicit or implied, appear to govern and colour this play. It must be admitted that they are just the ideas suited to the purpose of bringing about the alliance with Argos, or of cementing that alliance if, as is possible, it had already been made when the play was performed. Nor are all of them incompatible with the Euripides of whom his other plays speak to us. He was not, indeed, a patriot of the 'my country right or wrong' type; but still he was a patriot. To some foolish hotheads he might seem the enemy of Athens; but he was in truth like Eteoclus the Argive in this play, who, as he makes Adrastus say (ll. 878–80),

> ...bore
> To his country no ill will, only to her
> Bad citizens: for she is surely not
> To blame, if by the fault of evil guides
> Her fame is tarnished.

His hatred was not for the duped and misled people, but for the politicians who duped and misled it. Like other men he could feel a measure of pride in his country's fame and power and wealth. He had no reason to like Thebes, or to dislike Argos. He may even have thought the alliance with Argos a wise thing, worthy of his support: the play offers, as we shall see, some evidence that he did not, but it is at least possible that he did. He cannot have failed to share the resentment felt against Thebes for her refusal to surrender the Athenian dead after Delium. Neither such resentment nor support of the alliance would seem consistent with any attack, in this play, on the policy of Athens or on the ideals that underlay that policy. Such considerations might lead us to believe that Euripides in this play does mean what he appears to mean, and not something else. Yet there are things even in this play which are not easy to explain on this assumption, and which suggest that the critic and satirist is not, after all, on holiday. Let us first consider the feature that seems to point most clearly to this latter conclusion.

The *Troades* itself hardly lays more stress than the *Suppliants* lays on the horrible, foolish and futile nature of war. That Adrastus denounces war does not, to be sure, go for much. What he says of it may be thought no more than what is dramatically appropriate to the leader of a disastrously unsuccessful invasion. It is perhaps no clear sign, therefore, of any passionate hatred of war on the part of the poet himself when he makes Adrastus end the scene in which the remains of the dead chiefs are brought back from the field of battle with the words (ll. 949–54):

> Poor fools of men, why get you swords, and take
> The lives one of another? Nay, forbear:
> Cease ye from warfare, dwell ye quietly
> In peace and concord with your neighbour states.
> Life is a thing soon past: let it be spent
> As easily as it may, not crush'd by war.

Yet even here the wording, and the position, of the whole passage suggest that the poet is speaking for himself and not merely making Adrastus speak in character. Hardly less strong and significant is his denunciation of the folly of the Argives in choosing to settle their quarrel with the Thebans by fighting instead of by negotiation (ll. 744–9). More remarkable, because less dramatically appropriate, are the words of the Theban herald to Theseus (ll. 476–93):

> Bethink thee; nor because thou art king, forsooth,
> Of a free city, in anger with my words
> Give me a stout and saucy answer back.
> Hope is a traitor; often it hath embroiled
> Cities and raised them to excess of wrath.
> For the issue of war and peace once set before
> The popular vote, none looks for his own death,
> But thinks this fate will light on other men.
> If, at his voting, he saw death before him,
> War-madness would not be destroying Greece.
> And yet the better of the two arguments
> We all know, all distinguish good from bad,

See how much better is peace for man than war,
Peace, friend of the arts, hater of the powers of hate,
Who gives us wealth, and children in our homes:
All which we fools cast from us, to engage
In wars, city with city and man with man,
To make weak cities and weak men our slaves.

But the poet's hatred of war is expressed far more thoroughly than by these occasional open attacks on it. Nearly every utterance of the Chorus, which is made up of mothers of slain Argive warriors, declares their intense and hopeless misery in the bereavement that war has brought on them. This is especially marked after the Thebans are beaten and the dead bodies recovered. Till then, their sense of bereavement is mingled with the further agony of knowing their sons unburied and in the enemy's hands. For a little while the news of victory and rescue almost consoles them; but not for long. 'Thus much is well,' they cry, 'but the rest is misery' (l. 778); and from that moment, with an absorption in their own misery the effect of which is heightened by the equally complete absorption of Adrastus in his, every other feeling, even that of gratitude to Athens, is swallowed up in lonely and hopeless despair. Their misery is only intensified by the arrival of the remains of their sons' bodies, already so terribly disfigured that Theseus, in pity for the poor mothers, forbids them to see or touch those dreadful relics the recovery of which has for so long been their one object in life: they are only to take home the bones after the burning. In the last choral ode, to the renewed woe of the mothers there is added the woe of the slain men's little sons: in all the work of the great master of pathos there are few things, if any, more pitiful than this. The distress and desolation of Adrastus, throughout the play, is only less moving than that of the mothers and the children. The frenzied self-immolation of Euadne the widow of Capaneus is but another of the horrors that war brings forth. Some critics seem to find it an irrelevant piece of sensationalism; and if we are content with the ordinary view of the play's purpose, it *is* irrelevant. But to those who can see the play as the work of a bitter enemy of war and militarism, the bearing of this episode is plain. This is another of the fruits of war, that it drives hapless women stark mad, so that they kill themselves in the fantastic belief that thus they honour their dead. All they achieve is the greater misery of their kinsfolk who survive them; and the grief and despair of Euadne's old father Iphis, which might seem no less irrelevant than what precedes and causes it, has the same terrible relevance as the madness and suicide itself.

Τοιαῦθ' ὁ τλήμων πόλεμος ἐξεργάζεται

—such is the work of cruel war: that is the chief key to the meaning of this tragic and terrible play.

It may be replied that war is indeed an evil and terrible thing, but sometimes unavoidable, if worse evils are to be avoided; that this war which Theseus makes has a noble purpose, and achieves valuable results; that it is not one of those wars of which Theseus himself speaks (ll. 232–7), forced upon a country by blood-thirsty young men who are greedy for the military glory or political power or money that war will bring them, and are careless of the suffering it will cause to the mass of the people. But is even this war justified by its results? Rather in pity than in angry contempt, the poet seems to question the common belief that the burial of the dead is so vitally important a matter. Can it matter to the dead? That is nowhere suggested. Is it so great a boon to the living to be able to handle the bones that survive

the burning of the dead? Old Iphis at least is of another
mind (ll. 1104–7):

> Come now, delay not, lead me home, and there
> Shut me in darkness, that I may fast from food,
> Starve my old body, and waste away, and die.
> What shall it profit me to handle my son's bones?

Neither for the dead's sake nor for his own will he wait
to achieve, without trouble or risk, what the Argive
mothers were so eager to achieve that they were willing
to risk the destruction of an army for nothing else at all.
Thus even this seemingly noblest of wars is degraded to
the position of a piece of wasteful folly. Even with
victory, it has cost the Athenians many lives. We know
this, for the messenger's speech is no mere conventional
battle-piece. It stresses the physical horrors of combat;
and it insists on the obstinacy of the struggle, which went
on for a long time undecided, until at last—largely, we
gather, owing to the vigour with which Theseus swung
his club, breaking men's necks and mowing off their
heads (ll. 715–17)—at last the Thebans gave way.
A high price to pay for a few bones—and perhaps for
something else we will note later.

This line of argument may seem a little strained and
fanciful, though I believe it will bear examination. In
any case, there is another piece of anti-militarist satire
so bitter, and so slightly veiled, that it is strange how
completely it has apparently escaped notice. One of the
most heart-rending touches in that final chorus of
wailing mothers and crying children is the sudden outburst of the children (ll. 1143–7):

> Canst thou hear, O father,
> The cries of thy children?
> Shall thy son be a soldier
> One day, with a shield of his own?

> O may the day of vengeance come
> Upon them that struck thee down!
> It will come, if the gods so please—
> Revenge for my father's blood.

The words, as terrible as they are simple and natural, wring a fresh cry of agony from the poor mothers:

> Is the spirit of evil still at its work?
> Ah me, ill-fortune enough we have,
> Enough of sorrow and pain.

The boys pay no heed; the picture of revenge and victory has caught their fancy:

> Gleaming Asopus shall yet see me
> In brazen arms, to the fight
> Leading an Argive company
> To revenge for my father slain.

The boys' mood passes: they seem to see their fathers' silent ghosts before them, and grief for their loss overpowers the momentary vision of vengeance. The vision does not return: in what follows (ll. 1165–82) neither Theseus nor Adrastus speaks any word to encourage the notion of future revenge, nor makes any mention of such a thing. How should they, when Adrastus has admitted that the invasion was an act of ὕβρις no less than the recent behaviour of the Thebans (ll. 739–41):

> And Eteocles offered us fair conditions
> Of peace: we would not take them, and therefore we
> Were stricken.

No; but the play closes with a solemn injunction laid on the Argive boys to make a war of revenge, and it is spoken by Athena. Having seen and heard so much of what war and its consequences are, and remembering the frank confession of Adrastus that his invasion of

Thebes was unjust, now let us listen to the last words of the patron goddess of Athens (ll. 1213–26):

> This I bid *thee* do; and you Argive boys
> This: When ye are grown to manhood, go, lay waste
> The city of Thebes; for your dead fathers' blood
> Exact requital. Thou in thy father's stead
> Be their young captain, Aegialeus; and thou, O son
> Of Tydeus, come from thy Aetolian town
> To join him, thou to whom thy father gave
> The name of Diomedes. And as soon
> As the beards shall overshadow your cheeks shall ye
> Lead the mailed host of Argos to assault
> Thebes' seven-gated fortress. To their sorrow
> Shall ye, the full-grown whelps of the lion, come
> To sack their city. Thus surely it shall be.
> Hellas shall call you the Children of the Seven
> And after-ages celebrate your deeds
> In song, so valiant an army shall
> Ye lead to war, and heaven shall be with you.

Were these words penned by a satirist taking a holiday? Their effect is all the greater because they follow a long injunction to Theseus that is hardly less repulsive. Theseus has taken a courteous leave of Adrastus and the Argive mothers, expressing indeed the earnest hope that Argos will never forget what Athens has done for her, but leaving it at that, content with the simple promise of Adrastus, that Argive gratitude shall be lasting. With mutual good wishes for the future, they are about to go their several ways, when Athena appears, and speaks thus (ll. 1183–95):

> Theseus, hear thou Athena's words—what thou
> Shalt do, and doing shall serve thy country well.
> Give not these bones so lightly for these boys
> To carry to Argos: let them not go, until
> Thou hast exacted an oath in recompense
> Of all that Athens and thou have done for them.

105

This oath let Adrastus take, who, being king
Of Argos, has authority to take it
For all his people. And this shall be the oath:
That never shall the Argive host invade
This land in war; and if other enemies
Assail her, it shall fight in her defence.
Which oath if they forswearing come against
Athens, let ruin fall on Argos' land.

She continues with an account of the exact formalities to be observed in connexion with this oath. Thus the enterprise of a chivalrous nation and king, undertaken (in part at least) from unselfish motives of piety and pity, is degraded into a sordid bargain for the solid advantage of Athens. Not that most of the audience would see anything amiss in this; nor indeed in the following orders for a war of revenge; nor in the dutiful reply of Theseus (ll. 1227–31):

Gracious Athena, I will obey thy words;
For it is thou liftest me up, that I
Offend not. By this oath I will bind Adrastus.
Only be thou my guide: if Athens have
Thy favour, in safety shall we dwell for ever.

But are not the more enlightened invited to ask themselves whether this Athena is quite the deity a sensible and decent man would desire as his country's patron and director? Is it not her fault that Aethra, mother of Theseus, can hold up the ideal of Athens as a city full of pride, ready to take offence at any insult and to wipe it out in blood, and growing great by the wars she wages, unlike those quiet and cautious communities who never attempt or achieve anything distinguished (ll. 321–5)? We have an echo of this when the Theban herald levels at Theseus the not unfamiliar taunt (l. 576):

Thou art a meddler, and thy city too;

and Theseus replies:

> Great fighters are we, and therefore is our fortune
> Great also.

Do these words come from the poet's heart? Or is his real sympathy more with Adrastus in the words already quoted (ll. 950–2) that bid men cease from warfare and dwell in peace with their neighbours?

And if so, is not the apparent support of the treaty with Argos in effect an attack upon that treaty? Euripides, like many others, may not have discerned the aggressive intentions of its active advocates. But if he did, can we believe that he was in favour of it, and that he is genuinely recommending it here in the *Suppliants*, this play one of whose chief lessons is the *futility* of war?[1]

The way is perhaps now open for the entrance of some suspicion that the eulogy of the Athenians is not quite whole-hearted, not quite free from reservations in favour of other points of view, and from touches of satirical innuendo, meant to appeal to an intelligent and right-minded minority—if it was a minority—of the poet's audience and readers. We may by now feel uneasy about certain other aspects of the play, and be disposed to seek along the same lines for the explanation of some other facts that need explaining. It may be suggested in the first place that the portrait of Theseus is not quite what it has usually been taken to be. Not that he is a fool, a coward, or a knave. Euripides likes to put down the mighty from their seat, and to exalt the humble and meek; to whitewash traditional villains, and to blacken traditional heroes. But all with moderation:

---

[1] In this connexion I would invite attention to a possibly (not certainly) intentional *double entendre* in ll. 375–6:

> τί μοι πόλις κρανεῖ ποτ'; ἆρα φίλιά μοι
> τεμεῖ, καὶ τέκνοις ταφὰς ληψόμεσθα;

he does not turn the heroes into villains, or the villains into heroes, but tends rather to make them all stand on the level of humanity as we know it. They become rather ordinary men and women, with modest virtues and far from monstrous faults and failings: some better than others, but none wholly good or wholly bad, and many of them capable of sinking to great depths, or rising to great heights, under the influence of exceptional circumstances. The portrait of Theseus is no exception to this general rule. On the whole, he is a good fellow enough: a stout warrior certainly, and no shirker of duty. But we may discern some odd touches in the portrait. He is very ready to lecture the unhappy Adrastus, to show him just what a fool he has been, and why; and we may be inclined to sympathize with Adrastus' gentle but dignified protest (ll. 253–6):

> My lord, I chose thee not to be my judge,
> The chastener and correcter of the deeds
> I am found to have done amiss: I sought thy *help*.

The lecture Theseus delivers is full of complacent confidence in his own point of view, a quality that may be observed elsewhere in his utterances, though they are not always clear or logically coherent—this weakness is prominent in the lecture to Adrastus—and though they express very conventional ideas. When at last he has been persuaded to undertake the expedition against Thebes, he is very full of the righteousness of his cause, and talks impressively about the importance of maintaining Pan-hellenic custom and obeying the ancient ordinances of heaven. But it is in truth neither this, nor any pity for the unfortunate, that won his support. After some rather perfunctory words (ll. 301–3) about the religious obligation involved, his mother, who has from the first been on the side of the suppliant mothers, appeals at great

length to his concern for his own reputation as a warrior
and a brave man; and his own words (ll. 337–45) show
that he changes his mind because he is afraid of getting
the name of coward and weakling. In fact, he is not
without his share of vanity, moral and intellectual; and
he is, like most of us, capable of deceiving himself about
the real nature of his motives for action.

Again, like some other gentlemen of rank, he is not
above bullying his social inferiors. There is no good
ground for his repeated abuse of the Theban herald as
a windbag (ll. 426, 458–62, 567). His repudiation of the
title of τύραννος, and his laudation of the democracy
which he controls, somewhat incongruously, as monarch
(ll. 403–8), fully justify the not very lengthy criticism of
democracy with which the herald replies to his challenge
(ll. 409–25). He replies to that, in his turn, at double the
length of the herald's speech (ll. 426–56); and though the
herald's points are not met, and though the herald nevertheless courteously says, 'Well, let us agree to differ'
(ll. 465–6) and goes on to the business he came to do, yet
when, after another very long speech from Theseus, the
herald says, 'May I say just a word or two more in
conclusion?', Theseus once more taunts him with
loquacity (ll. 566–7). After a short exchange of defiance
and threats, Theseus cries, 'Your boasts shall not make
me lose my temper'—is it not lost already?—'get you
from this land, and take your foolish speeches with you'
(ll. 581–3). Too much may easily be made of all this; but
we can see that Theseus is deliberately set well below the
level of the heroic, and even, here and there, made a
little ridiculous.

To the same effect are two little touches not easily
explained as conventions of traditional Greek thought
or of dramatic usage. One is the self-importance of

Theseus when Adrastus is about to reply to the herald's demands (ll. 513–16):

> Hold thy peace, Adrastus!
> Silence! speak not till I have spoken: not
> To thee this herald comes: he comes to me,
> And it is I must answer him again.

The other touch is the priggish sententiousness of his departure with his mother (ll. 359–64):

> Set free my mother, that I may lead her hence
> To my father's house, leaning upon my arm
> Who love her. Ill betide the man too proud
> To be the slave of them whose son he is:
> Nobly-rewarded service—what he gives
> His parents, from his children he receives.

Other such touches might be cited: those mentioned are perhaps enough to show that Euripides has not suspended his customary practice of making his great men a little ordinary. No need, for his purpose, to go further; nor, if he had wished, could he have dared to make the national hero openly absurd. What he has done would not offend the average Athenian, or even be noticed, any more than the average Athenian would suspect satire in Athena's bloodthirsty injunction to the boys of Argos. But if we feel that the satire is none the less there for the discerning spectator to see, we shall feel all the more sure of this if we compare the portrait of Theseus with that of Demophon in the *Heraclidae*, where once again Athens and her king fight for the deliverance of the oppressed. The portrait of Demophon seems wholly free from all that we have been noting in the Theseus of the *Suppliants*.

Next we may look at the political implications of the play. The first part of the interview between Theseus and the Theban herald consists of an argument on the respective merits and defects of tyranny and democracy as forms of government. As Theseus is at least ostensibly the hero of the play, and as he defends democracy and attacks tyranny at considerable length, and is allowed to have the last word; as, further, the democratic Athenians are shown triumphant in battle over tyrant-governed Thebes: it is perhaps natural that critics have supposed Euripides to be laying aside, for this occasion, that hostile criticism of his country's system of government which he unmistakably offers us in other plays, and to be substituting a sincere eulogy of the existing constitution. But there are one or two reasons for doubting this, even if we grant, as we may, that for this occasion he is pretending to do so.

The herald puts forward just those objections to democracy which Euripides has clearly expressed or implied elsewhere: that the mass of the people have no time to become experts in the art of government, and are therefore controlled and misled by upstart demagogues, to the great disadvantage of decent citizens and of the country as a whole (ll. 409–25). Not only is this good Euripidean doctrine, but Theseus does little or nothing in his reply to meet these criticisms: what he does do is to draw a picture of freedom and equality under democracy which obviously goes beyond the actual facts, and which in any case does not attempt to show that freedom and equality are good for a country. He then goes on to draw a highly-coloured picture (ll. 442–55) of the horrors of an extreme tyranny of the worst sort, a picture likewise untrue to the actual facts, and not applicable, in any case, to the Thebes of the fifth century, whereas the herald's criticisms are only too fully applicable to contemporary Athens. Further, it is just the sort of troubles that beset contemporary Athens—the unscrupulous ambitions of leading politicians, the envy and malice of the poorer classes whom they control and mislead, and the consequent weakness of the middle class who are the backbone of the State—it is just these troubles which Theseus himself declares (ll. 232–45) have been the ruin of Argos and her king; and Argos, at the time of the Peace of Nicias, was and long had been a democracy.

Again, no attempt is made to account for the co-existence of democracy with the rule of Theseus as king. The consent of the people is not necessary for the war against Thebes: the decision plainly rests with Theseus alone. Having decided on war, 'I wish', he says, 'the city as a whole to approve my decision' (l. 349)—'wish', nothing more: δόξαι δὲ χρήҙω καὶ πόλει πάσῃ τόδε. He adds, with complete confidence, 'and they will, if I wish it', δόξει δ' ἐμοῦ θέλοντος, 'but I shall keep them in a better temper if I allow them a say in the matter', ἀλλὰ τοῦ λόγου προσδοὺς ἔχοιμ' ἂν δῆμον εὐμενέστερον. His confidence turns out, of course, to be justified (ll. 393–4):

> And willingly and readily the folk
> Consented to this war, so soon as they
> Knew it to be my will.

Not so much difference, after all, between Argos headed into war by her young politicians eager for power, command, glory or money, and Athens going to war because, and as soon as, her warlike young king finds war necessary—on second thoughts—for the protection of his honour as a brave man and a soldier. Quite probably Euripides is glancing at the practically despotic power Pericles had enjoyed, and also, perhaps more emphatically, at the power the charming and popular Alcibiades was beginning to enjoy in his turn. But this is not encomium: it is the political satirist at work. And here again he might feel safe with his

audience. However complete the sway exercised by a
demagogue over a mob, the mob will always believe
itself his master, not his dupe and his tool. Is there not
a rather pretty *double entendre* in Theseus' boast (ll. 352–3):

καὶ γὰρ κατέστησ' αὐτὸν [i.e. τὸν δῆμον] εἰς μοναρχίαν
ἐλευθερώσας τήνδ' ἰσόψηφον πόλιν?

Ostensibly this means: 'I enthroned the *demos* as sole
sovereign when I set this land free and made its people
equal.' But it might mean: 'I reduced the *demos* to sub-
jection to one man's rule when I (nominally) set this land
free and made its people equal.' 'One man one vote'
may well lead to one man in full power.

What has so far been said has prepared us to find the
treatment of religion not wholly free from irony. The
piety of Theseus, which is stressed in several places, is
doubtless in itself an estimable quality; but it is less
attractive when the divine objects of it are shown to be
unworthy of reverence and obedience. When Athena's
cruel speech to the Argive boys is immediately followed
by Theseus' words of complete trust in her and devotion
to her (ll. 1227–31), the intelligent and humane spectator
may feel that Theseus might with advantage have had
less piety, and more intelligence and humanity. Here,
as elsewhere, Euripides shows himself not irreligious, not
a frivolous scoffer at divine power, but so truly religious
as to deplore the misdirection of his countrymen's
religious instincts, and to seek to direct those instincts to
worthier objects. Consider, again, the last words of
Theseus before he goes off to fight Thebes (ll. 594–7):

> I have need
> Of one thing only, the help of all the gods
> Who care for justice. This is the ally
> That gives men victory: valour is naught
> For such as have not God's goodwill with them.

Certainly: but we see by the time the play is over that Athena's care for justice leaves something to be desired. And we have found some reason to doubt whether it is well that religion should support a war made merely to recover dead bodies for burial, a war which, however successful, means the loss of more human lives, and if unsuccessful merely multiplies the original disaster. There is a terrible unconscious irony in the words of the Chorus (ll. 778–85) when their short-lived joy at the news of victory has given way before their returning sense of desolation and misery:

> Good and evil are joined together:
>> To the glory of Athens' name
> Glory accrues, fresh fame is added
>> To her great captain's fame:
> But to us there is given the sight of our dead sons'
>> limbs,
> This sight of beauty and pain, if indeed it befall
> That we see them, and see this day that we looked
>> not for,
>> This grief that is greater than all.

Double glory for Athens and for Theseus: for the poor mothers, the sharpest of all agonies. Well, religion tells us the dead must be buried, at all costs: all Greece believes this is the will of God. Yet not old Iphis only, but the mothers themselves at times, feel how little it really matters. They were alive and now are dead; we have lost them, lost them for ever, and life holds nothing worth our having henceforward: that is the great fact, all that really matters, and religion has nothing to say to it—except to command and predict another bloody war in a few years' time. Would not the wish of Adrastus, that men should disarm and dwell at peace in their own lands, be more likely to be fulfilled if Athena Promachos and her like were less to the fore, and the living less readily sacrificed to the dead at the behest of a superstition that brings no benefit either to the dead or to the living?

The Delphic oracle and the custom of divination by sacrifice are not very prominent in this play; and in spite of Euripides' well-known hostility to both, it is perhaps only in the light of considerations already advanced that we should be led to expect irony in his few references to them. But in that light we may smile a little at the conclusion of Theseus' long list of the blessings bestowed by heaven on ungrateful man (ll. 211–15):

> And things uncertain and obscure to us
> Diviners prophesy, who scan the fire,
> The folded entrails, and the flight of birds.
> Are we not dainty, if God so decks our life
> With blessings and we are not satisfied?

We may also wonder whether the folly of Adrastus really lay in disregarding the warnings of the diviners against the expedition of the Seven (ll. 155–9, 229–31), and not rather, or only, in yielding to the war-party in Argos (ll. 232–3):

> Led astray
> By the counsel of young men athirst for posts
> Of honour, stirrers-up of unjust war.

And while we may congratulate the Delphic oracle on arranging the marriage of Aethra to Aegeus (ll. 6–7) and so bringing about the birth of Theseus, we may be less ready to approve its wisdom in bidding Adrastus marry his two daughters to a boar and a lion. Theseus, to be sure, blames not the oracle but Adrastus for the disastrous consequences. The passage in which he does so (ll. 219–28) is curiously obscure. Taken as it stands,

it implies at first sight not merely that Adrastus was a fool
to marry his daughters to the two blood-stained and ill-
starred fugitives Tydeus and Polynices, but that he was
a fool to do so in obedience to the oracle, θεσφάτοις
Φοίβου ζυγείς, 'as though the gods really existed', ὡς
ζώντων θεῶν, an expression that seems incredible in
the mouth of the pious Theseus.[1] Whatever we are to
make of this difficulty, it seems plainly hinted by the
poet that this particular Delphic utterance is not a happy
instance of the benefits conferred by divination in
enabling us to understand 'the things uncertain and
obscure to us', but rather must be held responsible for
all the unhappy sequel. Theseus does not suggest how
Adrastus ought to have interpreted the oracle, if indeed
his fault lay in misinterpreting it and not in obeying it.
We seem to be left with a choice between supposing that
Adrastus interpreted the oracle correctly but was a fool
to obey it, and supposing that he interpreted it wrongly.
The latter view fits better the preceding lines (216–18),
in which ungrateful men are said to be led by their
conceit into fancying themselves wiser than the gods.
But this would suggest that when Apollo prescribed
a boar and a lion as Adrastus' sons-in-law he meant just
what he said, and that Adrastus should have carried out
his instructions literally. I must leave the problem of the
passage unsolved; but that *some* satire is directed against
Delphi seems clear. Such satire, even if perceived by the
audience generally, might not give much offence: the
pro-Spartan tendencies of the oracle during the war, we
know, made it unpopular at Athens, and not everyone
would see that the misconduct of Apollo's contemporary

[1] Perhaps the true reading is δόντων (or ἐώντων) θεῶν: this would
remove the immediate difficulty of these three words, but would not
clear up the passage as a whole.

ministers had nothing to do with his trustworthiness in days long past.

One or two other passages concerning religion may be noticed, which might indeed have given offence if their satirical intention had been generally perceived, but which were no doubt not thus understood by most people. One of these is the remark of Theseus (ll. 925–7) that Amphiaraus needs no such eulogy from Adrastus as he has given to five out of the Seven, for *him* the gods

> Bore hence alive with chariot and horses
> To the earth's deep caves, and thus plainly themselves
> Pronounce his eulogy.

This conveys a plain hint to the discerning spectator, both that the alleged miracle is a fiction, and that, even if it were a fact, the eulogy implied by it is equivocal. That it is not a convincing testimonial to Amphiaraus would be noted by those who remembered how the Theban herald interpreted it (ll. 500–1) as one piece of evidence that the Argive invaders were in the wrong and justly punished by their defeat (l. 505). Another pretty touch is the division of opinion amongst the anxious Chorus, while the result of the battle is still unknown, about whether the gods are indeed just or not, and whether they can or cannot be trusted to reward the righteous and punish the wicked: whereas when the news of victory has come, the Chorus-leader cries (ll. 731–2):

> Now that we have seen a happier day than we
> Dared hope for, now we have faith in God.

They are not the only good folk whose faith in the justice of heaven depends on what happens to themselves.

The interpretation of the *Suppliants* offered in this chapter will not be readily welcomed unless the general view of the plays of Euripides which it implies is to some extent accepted: the view, namely, that we are to recognize in them the frequent recurrence of satirical criticism, the effect of which is to reverse or deny at least some part of what appears on the surface. If no such view be accepted of the plays in general, or even of certain plays, such as the *Ion*, the *Heracles*, and the *Bacchae*, about which such a view should be true if it is true of any of the plays, it will certainly seem much less likely to be true in the single case of the *Suppliants*. But if such a view is accepted regarding all or most of the other plays, there will be good reason to hold that the *Suppliants* is no exception to the general rule. What has been said in this chapter is intended to show that, despite first appearances to the contrary, the *Suppliants* is not exceptional, but falls well into line with a number of the other plays. Like them, it contains clear indications that the poet's real views and feelings on certain matters are hidden—and yet revealed to the discerning—under a surface display of views that he does not take and of feelings that he does not feel. It is not, to those who look below this surface, a glorification of Athens as an imperial military power; not an ideal painting of the great Athenian hero; not a vindication of Athenian democracy or a defence of orthodox Athenian religion: none of these things either primarily or incidentally. 'The play is an encomium of the Athenians.' Perhaps; but perhaps those who are offered their choice of eulogists from among the immortals should think twice before choosing Euripides.

The bearing of my interpretation of the *Suppliants* on the 'fantasy' theory maintained in my first three chapters is not negligible, though somewhat general and indirect. Except for a few not very important details, the story of the play is credible throughout. It is not one of those which represent events that did not and could not have happened. The few supernatural features that it includes, of which the theophany at the end is the only one actually represented, are not essential parts of it. Because they are nevertheless there, they must be explained somehow, either as I would explain all such features, or in some other fashion. But they present no special problem. Whatever explanation of them most commends itself in those plays where they are an integral and unremovable part of the story can easily be applied to them in this play, where they are not. In this particular respect, the *Suppliants* neither supports the 'fantasy' theory, nor needs it at all seriously in order itself to be understood.

None the less, understood as I understand it, the play does give support, and strong support, to the 'fantasy' theory. What will probably most discourage acceptance of that theory is a general preliminary reluctance to allow that Euripides not only could have disbelieved in the credibility of the stories he presented, but could have taken pains to indicate that disbelief to those who were able to perceive what he meant. Yet here in the *Suppliants*, if I am right, he is doing something else of much the same kind. He is professing to uphold certain political, moral and religious principles and policies which he not only does not uphold, but takes pains to indicate that he does not. In both cases alike, we may say that he is saying one thing and meaning another; or, as Verrall from his rather different point of view would prefer to put it, that he is meaning one thing while making a decorous pretence of meaning another. It seems reasonable, therefore, to hold that my interpretation of the *Suppliants*, owing nothing to the 'fantasy' theory, and strengthened by many parallel instances of a similar procedure in many other plays, goes some way to support the 'fantasy' theory, not so much by bringing forward any positive argument in its favour as by removing one of the major inducements to reject it. Because of the *Suppliants*, there is less plausibility in the view that Euripides *could* not have behaved as, on other grounds, my thesis maintains that he did; and all the less because hitherto the *Suppliants* has almost wholly escaped the suspicion of double-dealing.

CHAPTER V

REALISM AND GREEK TRAGEDY

The slightest acquaintance with the tragedy of ancient
Greece is enough to show how different it is from any
type of drama recognized and established in modern
Europe. It is different in external form, in material
content, and in the relation between form and content.
Since all who are able to study it begin with at least some
knowledge of modern drama and the modern theatre,
they are apt, in the earlier stages of that study, to be
perplexed and even discouraged by these differences.
Increasing familiarity steadily dispels their perplexity
and discouragement. What seemed strange to them
comes to seem natural, and what repelled them they now
find attractive. They can now encourage the learner to
expect, they can even in some measure enable him to
share, the understanding and pleasure they have already
achieved for themselves. Something like this is probably
a matter of common experience for those whose studies
have lain this way.

  Now while such persons will probably agree that it is
helpful to them to know something of modern drama
and the theatre of today, and that the more of such
knowledge they have the better they can deal with the
drama of ancient Greece, yet they do not as a rule
perceive that such knowledge brings with it a danger of
its own. Undoubtedly a help, it may also be a hindrance.
Those who are acquainted with any two forms of art
between which any degree of kinship exists are often
disposed to overestimate the resemblances between the

two, and to underestimate the differences; and they are more likely to do so if they seek to enlighten, regarding one of such forms of art, those who know little or nothing about it but are more or less familiar with the other. There is some reason to think that this tendency has done something to hinder, as well as to forward, the just appreciation of Greek tragedy in our own day. It has indeed aroused interest not easily to be aroused otherwise, and given profound pleasure that could perhaps be given only thus; and the harm that has accompanied this great good may seem trivial. It may seem to consist in no more than being misled on certain matters of detail, in errors which the professional scholar should and can avoid, but which only pedants would deplore as grievously injurious to anyone else.

Were this true, perhaps no more need be said. But the harm extends further. It most affects those who feel a special interest in our own drama, as readers or playgoers, it may be as producers or actors. Even mature scholars are misled by such interest into regarding ancient drama too much from the point of view of a present-day dramatic critic; into requiring and expecting from ancient drama just what they rightly require and expect from modern drama; and consequently into finding what is not there to be found, and failing to find what is. And the learner who follows their lead, in most respects to his great advantage, is nevertheless led to adopt what is wrong in their outlook, and may easily exaggerate it. It might be wiser to stress more, even at the outset, the differences between the two forms of art, and to dwell less on their resemblances. The resemblances will easily suggest themselves: the differences, if ignored or minimized, have a way of obtruding themselves none the less which is puzzling and displeasing, and which is best avoided by facing them boldly and fully recognizing their existence.

With most of these differences the regular student of Greek tragedy is familiar. But often he seems to be aware of them only as isolated facts. He does not perceive, or at least he does not perceive clearly, that from most or all of them, considered together, we are bound to infer that the ancient Greek conception of what a drama should be is different, in at least one important respect, from that which prevails in modern Europe. Because he does not perceive this, he is apt to criticize and interpret Greek plays on principles which may safely and rightly be employed in dealing with modern plays, but which cannot be safely or rightly applied to those of ancient Greece. He will lay it down that this or that which would beyond question be a serious blemish in a modern play must be not less so in an ancient play; that what could not be done today by any good playwright could not have been done by any good playwright then; that there are canons of dramatic propriety universally applicable, and that any critic who rejects these, or fails to apply them to Greek drama, simply condemns himself. Such an attitude is especially likely to be adopted by those who, besides being deeply interested in modern drama, have zealously concerned themselves with the production of ancient drama on the modern stage: in their most laudable attempt to maximize its appeal to modern audiences, the tendency to assimilate the dissimilar is not easy for them to resist. But the tendency is not confined to them: it is general, if not universal, among all serious students of classical literature.

Before discussing some of the differences between ancient and modern drama that are well recognized, and one other that seems hitherto to have escaped notice, I will indicate briefly the main distinction between the general conceptions of drama, in ancient and modern times, to which these differences clearly point and to which they are clearly due. In doing so, I shall be thinking and speaking of ancient drama as represented by tragedy, and of modern drama as represented by those forms of it which in spirit and purpose are most akin to ancient tragedy. I shall not consider how far the same distinction holds good as between Greek satyr drama and comedy on the one hand, and modern comedy, farce and the like on the other hand. It can, I think, be shown to hold good here too on the whole, but I am not now concerned to prove that it does.

The distinction of which I speak may be expressed in a word or two by saying that ancient drama was not realistic. It did not attempt to produce in the spectators' minds any sort of illusion, any feeling, however temporary, that they were seeing and hearing what, in the distant past, actually took place. What was shown on the stage did not aim at *reproducing* the setting and the events of the old story, but at *suggesting* or *evoking* them. It helped and stimulated the spectators' imaginations so that they could and did picture to themselves the real scene and the real events, perceiving these through the medium, as it were, of what the eye actually saw and the ear actually heard. Just as the recitation of an epic by a single rhapsode, in which illusion was plainly impossible and was in no way attempted, could nevertheless cause the hearer to imagine vividly the scene and the various persons acting and speaking, so drama could do this; and this was all it did, all it could do, and all it sought to do. I would press this comparison between recited epic and drama as most valuable for the just

appreciation of the latter. A Greek drama was in essence
a recitation by several rhapsodes instead of by one: a
Greek recited epic was in essence a drama played by
a single actor instead of by several. Recited epic had
obvious advantages which drama lacked, and was
subject to obvious limitations from which drama was
free. But the effect of both alike depended on their
enabling the audience to imagine vividly a reality,
a sequence of words and deeds, which was not literally
and exactly reproduced by either, but merely evoked or
suggested.

We need consider no more than the externals of an
ancient performance of drama to convince ourselves
that realistic illusion was impossible. For at least half
a century, and probably for longer, there was no scenery,
apart from a permanent architectural background which
had to represent a temple front in one play and a palace
front in another, and in others again to be ignored
altogether. When 'scenographia' was introduced,
possibly quite late in the fifth century—we know only
that Aristotle assigns its introduction to Sophocles[1]—it
must have been a rough and simple affair as compared
with what is available for the most modest production
in any modern theatre. Can we suppose there was so
thorough a change of scenery in the *Eumenides* that an
unimaginative spectator would forthwith feel himself
looking at the Areopagus instead of at the temple of
Delphi? or such a presentation of the Caucasus moun-
tains in the *Prometheus*, or of the rocky shore of Lemnos
in the *Philoctetes*, as would do more than symbolize the
scene and prevent the regular background from con-
fusing and misleading the audience? Consider how little
the *eccyclema* could meet the most modest demand for

[1] Aristotle, *Poetics* 1449a 18.

realistic effect: so little, that no modern producer would risk the laughter that would attend its use, unless before an audience whose interest in the production was wholly antiquarian and undramatic. The action of the *Rhesus* takes place in the dead of night, and the characters grope their way through the darkness; but there was nothing except the actors' words and actions to tell the audience so. How little such considerations deterred the playwrights the *Eumenides*, *Prometheus* and *Rhesus* prove; had a maximum of realism in the matter of scenic surroundings been felt important, plays that make such extreme demands on the imagination would not have been written.

The equipment of the actors themselves tells the same story. The use of masks is quite incompatible with such realism as we have on the stage today. In real life, and therefore in a realistic play, changes of facial expression may matter as much as the words spoken, and sometimes more. The masked actor can use no such means of interpretation: if he is to convey the notion of anger or pity, hope or despair, happiness or misery, he must tell us—and often he tells us in so many words—that these are his feelings. Whether such a dramatist as Euripides would have welcomed the innovation of maskless actors we can only guess. The question simply did not arise. Masks were necessary, and plays were written to suit masked actors; and plays could suit masked actors only by not being realistic. In the same way, the actor's buskins and long trailing robes prevented the quick movements and delicate nuances of bodily gesture which the modern actor employs. The very costumes were strictly conventional. When Euripides clothed his exiled Telephus in rags instead of the rich garments appropriate to his rank, this mild approach to realism, which would today be a matter of course, was received with hostile derision;[1] so might a minister of religion be received today if he sought to illustrate the meaning of Ash Wednesday or Good Friday by officiating in a torn and dirty surplice. The hostility may have sprung from mere unintelligent conservatism; but also, and perhaps chiefly, from a sound instinctive feeling that where the imagination must in any case do so much it had better do all—that no realism is better than just a little. We might well feel today that Shakespeare, for instance, is better acted on a bare stage than with a few scenic accessories that can create no illusion and by their ludicrous inadequacy must hinder rather than help the spectators' imagination.

Realism was not less prevented by the regular practice of distributing all the character parts among three actors and no more. This practice was obviously not in itself unavoidable: it could and would have been abandoned, sooner or later, had there been any conscious desire for the greater realism to be got by assigning each part to a separate actor. But masks and costume were enough, with the help of the spoken word where necessary, to inform the audience of the actor's change of character; and having this information, the audience were content. We do not know if the actor changed or tried to change his voice with his part: there is nothing to show that he did, or that his doing so would not have been thought as absurd an innovation as the rags of Telephus. The poet's diction is the same for man and woman, for young and old, for free man and slave: why should the actor's voice not be the same also? In any case, no change of voice could ever fully disguise the identity of the actor; and why should it? Why may not

[1] So we may fairly gather from Aristophanes, *Acharnians*, ll. 430–64.

the king speak with the same voice as the king's daughter in the scene before, if there is no need for us to fancy that we are actually seeing and hearing the king now and were actually seeing and hearing his daughter then?

When we turn from the external to the internal features of a Greek tragedy, from those which have to do with its stage performance, and affect spectators only, to those which are equally the concern of the reader, the absence of realism is not less apparent. That the whole of every tragedy is in verse surprises us less than it might if our own literature had not accustomed us to a verse drama which is at least more realistic than that of Greece, if less so than that of today. We do not, therefore, perceive readily that its survival in Greek drama long after the development of many types of prose literature, and in particular of the prose dialogue with its purely dramatic form combined with its realism of spirit and content, is one important proof of the non-realistic nature of the drama. Any considerable advance towards realism on the stage would have led, sooner or later, to the substitution of prose for verse.

But tragedy is not only in verse; it is in verse whose rhythm and diction are never varied to express the variety in the characters who speak it. The slave, even the foreign slave, cannot be distinguished from his Greek master by the style of his utterance; and the youngest child is made to speak just like an adult, with results as grotesque, to the modern reader, as the look of a Jacobean monument, where graduated rows of sons and daughters reproduce in miniature the figure and costume of their parents. The choral odes, moreover, and the lyric monodies, even when their subject-matter clearly excludes the notion of something composed and learnt beforehand, and indicates the spontaneous reaction of the singers to unforeseen circumstances, are highly artificial in their formal structure. This is especially true of the metrical correspondence of strophe and anti-strophe, a feature not found in English verse drama at any time, apart from deliberate imitations of the Greek dramatic form; could anything be less compatible with realism?

So, too, with stichomythia, a form of dialogue that recurs in every play as regularly as versicles and responses in Christian liturgical services. It seems relatively natural to us when it is used for the quick verbal exchanges of persons quarrelling with each other or plotting eagerly together. But even here the undeviating regularity of the one line at a time, continued sometimes for forty lines or more without a break, is impossible in real life or in any drama that aims at producing the illusion of real life. And further, stichomythia is often used where such quick exchanges would not, in real life, occur at all, but one person would speak continuously, and the other either listen in silence or at most interpose a brief ejaculation now and then. The *Medea* offers a good instance of this (ll. 662–708): here we have Aegeus informing Medea of the reason for his having come to Corinth, and then Medea informing Aegeus of her present distressing plight; realism would make each of them in turn listen quietly to the other's tale, and not reply line by line, sometimes even taking the next words out of the narrator's mouth. Whatever the reason for the use of stichomythia in this and many similar passages (the purpose is possibly to convey that eager interest, on the part of the listener, which mask and costume made it impossible to convey by facial expression and bodily movements), it is clearly a thing which a realistic playwright would avoid.

Other instances of this ritualistic formalism of verbal expression will occur to the reader: it is needless, here, to attempt a complete list of them. We may turn to consider certain aspects of the use of the Chorus which reinforce the conclusion I am advocating. We might almost say that one of these is the simple fact of its continued existence. In a few plays, such as the *Suppliants* and *Eumenides* of Aeschylus and the *Suppliants* of Euripides, it is an essential element in the story, a true *dramatis persona*, if not the chief one. In some others, its presence and activity are at least natural and dramatically valuable, at certain points if not through-out. But in many others the modern reader is apt to feel that it is neither natural nor valuable, and that it would be better away; and so long as he continues to regard a Greek tragedy as a would-be reproduction of actual life, he must, in these plays at least, continue to feel thus about the Chorus. But once he ceases to think of a tragedy in this way, this feeling about the Chorus weakens and disappears. He is now ready to see some-thing in the view that the Chorus is not, as a rule, in the full sense a *dramatis persona*, but also forms part of the audience, witnessing the action as the audience does, rather than (or, at least, as well as) taking part in the action as the actors do; and that one of its functions is to express for the audience the feelings which the play-wright would have the audience entertain. He can now understand why it remains present, usually if not always, throughout the play, even when the action of the play covers days or even weeks: its functions are only inter-mittently dramatic; and in the intervals we need not expect it to leave the orchestra any more than we now expect the audience to leave the auditorium. He can now accept readily the convention by which the choral ode between two episodes may be understood to cover a very long interval of time, whereas seldom if ever does the supposed lapse of time during an episode differ greatly from the time actually occupied in the stage performance. He will now not find it strange that the Chorus—again like the audience—is permitted to see and hear the true *dramatis personae* say and do what in real life they would never say and do in the presence either of such persons as the Chorus or of anyone else. And in the removal of these and other like difficulties he will see further proof that realism is no part of the ancient conception of tragedy.

All these features of tragic form are likely to strike and to perplex the novice, just because to him they are novelties; especially if he knows a good deal about modern drama, in which, roughly speaking, such things do not occur. The more experienced scholar, on the other hand, has become so well used to them that he tends to overlook their significance, as he overlooks that of other differences between Greek drama and our own. He approaches the position of the Greek public for which the plays were written and performed, a public which, knowing nothing of any other drama, could have no notion that any other way of doing things was even possible. There is, however, at least one peculiar feature in the structure of a Greek tragedy with which it cannot be said that even experienced scholars are familiar, and which deserves some special attention, not only because of its importance for the matter we are now considering, but also because it has, if I am not mistaken, as yet escaped notice.

In nearly every tragedy we find, besides the choral odes, other lyrical passages, which are part of the episodes in which they occur, and are delivered wholly or mainly by one of the actors; and following these, and forming part of the same episodes, there are often monologues or dialogues in iambic verse, spoken wholly or mainly by the same actor as before, *during which, and by means of which, the position of affairs is not materially changed, and the action of the play does not go forward.* In such cases, spoken verse is resumed only to be the vehicle of a further response or reaction of the person concerned to the same situation as before; the whole episode may even end with no development in the action of the play. This further response or reaction is, on the whole and as a rule, more rational and intellectual, less purely emotional, than that already expressed in the lyrical passage: it tells us more of what the speaker thinks, less of what he feels. But this is all that is new: there are no fresh events. Of such sequences the surviving tragedies provide some twenty-five well-marked instances, besides some others less definitely of this particular type. Two very clear instances may be briefly noted, one in the *Oedipus Tyrannus* and one in the *Medea*.

In the former, when Oedipus comes forth blinded, we have first a lyrical monody with short responses by the Chorus (ll. 1307–68). This is followed by a long speech (ll. 1369–1415), which shows clearly the typical addition, in this spoken sequel, of thought, one might almost say of rational argument, to the more purely emotional reaction conveyed by the lyrics. But there is no change in the situation, no development of the action, until we reach the last seven lines (1409–15), the appeal in which ('hide me, slay me, cast me forth') prepares us for the arrival of Creon and the scene between him and Oedipus.

In the *Medea* (ll. 96–266), what may be called a lyric trio (Medea, Nurse, Chorus) is followed by a long speech from Medea. Both parts of this sequence—up to the appeal in the last eight lines of the speech, which, like the appeal in the *Oedipus* passage, does prepare us for what follows—have the same purpose, to show Medea's reaction to the desperate situation which the Nurse has already described in the prologue. But the tone of the speech—balanced, rational, calculating—is in startling contrast to the wild helpless despair of the lyrical utterances that have preceded it.

Careful consideration of these two passages and no more would perhaps be enough to reveal the quality, common to them all, to which I wish to draw attention. However, there are certain differences between the two that somewhat obscure this common quality, which will stand out quite clearly only if we examine a number of further examples of the same sequence. It may therefore be well to give a complete list of all the examples I have noted:

AESCHYLUS	*Prometheus*	88–192 : 193–276
		561–608 : 609–876
	Agamemnon	1072–1177 : 1178–1330
SOPHOCLES	*Ajax*	208–56 : 263–332
		333–429 : 430–80
	Antigone	806–81 : 883–928
	Oedipus Tyrannus	1297–1368 : 1369–1415
	Oedipus Coloneus	117-253 : 258–91
	Trachiniae	971–1043 : 1046–1111
	Electra	86–250 : 254–309
EURIPIDES	*Medea*	96–212 : 214–66
	Hippolytus	58–72 : 72–87
		177–266 : 267–309
		672–9 : 680–731
	Alcestis	243–79 : 280–368
		861–934 : 935–61
	Troades	308–41 : 343–405
		572–603 : 606–700

EURIPIDES	*Helena*	164–251: 254–329
	Bacchae	1169–99: 1202–15
	Phoenissae	301–54: 357–442
		1539–80: 1584–1614
	Rhesus[1]	1–51: 52–75
		728–55: 756–803
		890–914: 915–49

How are we to interpret these sequences in respect of their dramatic psychology? Commentators, naturally enough, take them at their face value. They suppose that the change of tone which undeniably marks the transition to the second part of each of these passages signifies a corresponding change, occurring at that point, in the thoughts and feelings of the speaker: that, for instance, Medea, in the passage noted above, 'pulls herself together', becomes more calm and collected and rational. It may seem absurd to question this view: the more so because in no single case, considered by itself, is the mental change clearly improbable. Yet there is reason to think this view mistaken. No other is possible so long as we interpret the plays realistically; no other could be conveyed, or even faintly suggested, by a stage performance to a modern audience; and it is only when we give up the realist attitude, and neglect the interests of the modern producer, that we shall be ready to admit the difficulty of accepting what may seem the judgement of plain common sense.

What makes this common-sense view untenable? Simply this: that while this type of sequence is, as we have seen, so usual as to occur at least once in a full half of the extant tragedies, *the reverse sequence does not occur*. The change of tone is always from the more agitated to

---

[1] Whether the *Rhesus* is the work of Euripides or not does not matter in the present context.

the more tranquil, from the more emotional to the more rational: never in the other direction. I do not mean that we never find, within the same episode, the transition from speech to song, from iambic to lyric verse. This is not uncommon. But whenever it occurs, it is because something fresh and exciting has happened to provoke it: a good instance is in the scene between Theseus and the Chorus in the *Hippolytus* (ll. 790–898), where two such transitions occur, the first provoked by the sight of Phaedra's corpse, and the second by the reading of her letter. So long as the situation remains unchanged, no such transition is found. To this rule there are a few seeming exceptions, but these may all be explained away by one of two considerations, or by both at once. Either the situation, though superficially the same, really does change: thus Iphigenia's lyric farewell to life before she goes off to be sacrificed (*Iphigenia in Aulide*, ll. 1475 ff.) is the first active step taken to carry out her heroic resolution, as opposed to the discussion and argument that preceded it. Or the lyric passage is anapaestic in metre, and therefore less markedly and undeniably lyric in tone than if other lyric metres had been used: this is well illustrated by the opening scene of the same play, where the two anapaestic duologues, ll. 1–48 and 115–63, have hardly any lyric quality about them. In several of Euripides' plays (*Medea, Troades, Electra, Bacchae, Phoenissae*) there are lyric passages immediately following spoken dialogue; but all of them accompany the beginning of a sorrowful departure, which is in effect a new piece of action, and three of the five are in anapaestic metre. It seems true that nowhere at all do we find spoken iambics at once followed by sung lyrics that represent a further response of the same persons to the same position of affairs.

This absence of the iambic-lyric sequence, coupled with the frequency of the lyric-iambic sequence, obliges us to regard the latter as a *convention*, as one of the many set forms which combine to make the whole shape of a Greek tragedy what it is. For if it were meant to signify, with some degree of realism, an actual and corresponding change of mental attitude in the speaker, there is nothing to account for the change being always in that direction and never in the other. *A priori*, it is at least as likely that such a change of mental attitude should be in the other direction, from the more rational and less emotional to the less rational and more emotional; at least as likely that a given personage should 'get worked up' and 'lose control of himself' as that he should 'calm down' and 'pull himself together', even when nothing fresh or exciting has occurred. Indeed, such changes of mental attitude *are* often represented. But they are never embodied in the iambic-lyric sequence that would appear to us the natural embodiment to give them.

We must conclude, then, that the lyric-iambic sequence is a pure formal convention. As such, it is not stranger or less credible than many others whose conventional character no one would question. We have seen, for instance, that stichomythia is often so thoroughly unnatural from any realistic point of view that its very strangeness forces us to recognize it as the convention which it undoubtedly is. Because the stichomythia convention is familiar to us, we notice its strangeness too little: because the lyric-iambic convention is unfamiliar, we may think it stranger than it really is.

It may indeed be admitted that this convention is a fact, and yet maintained that it is not quite such as

I take it to be. I take it to be a *literary* convention, a matter of pure external form that need not prevent us, and did not prevent the Greek spectator or reader, from recognizing the reality that underlies it. But it might be argued that the conventionality goes deeper, and applies to the actual psychology of the *dramatis personae* themselves: that they were regularly thought of, and *therefore* depicted, as being first excited and emotional and then more calm and rational. It is not easy to prove that such a way of looking at the matter is wrong. But fortunately there is little reason to think it right. Fortunately; for if we had to adopt it, it would inevitably lessen our admiration of Greek tragedy. We should be obliged to admit that the picture of human behaviour presented by tragedy was in one quite definite respect false and misleading—false to essential facts of human nature. However, there is no reason to attribute to Greek tragedy this more fundamental kind of conventionality, either in the matter we are now considering or in any other. And one good reason, perhaps the best reason, for trying to discover and emphasize the conventional character of its outward shape is that the more clearly we can perceive this the more clearly we can perceive the truth and reality of its inner substance.

What, then, is the reality that underlies this particular convention of the lyric-iambic sequence? To this question I am not sure that I can give the right answer. For my main purpose in this chapter, it does not matter much whether the question is or is not answered rightly, or answered at all. I have sought to prove the conventional character of this sequence in order to provide one more proof of the non-realistic character of Greek tragedy; and for this purpose it is enough to do what I hope I have done already. Nevertheless, the question is worth trying to answer; and my answer, right or wrong, is something like this. To reach the reality which the outward form here suggests, we have only to ignore the time-order presented to us, and to take all else as it stands. What is conveyed to us by the sung lyrics is to be mentally fused, as it were, with what is conveyed to us by the spoken iambics. The resultant complex will give us the psychological facts, the total reaction to the situation, rational and emotional, of the personage concerned, more fully and justly than either part of the sequence, considered in isolation, could give these facts. Thus neither Medea's wild cries of despair within the house, nor the logical exposition of her woes which she gives the Chorus, would afford, if considered separately, a true and complete picture of her state of mind at any moment; the two taken together do afford such a picture. If the order of the two elements of the sequence were reversed, the result would be exactly the same. They are in fact never thus reversed: the established conventional form is always maintained. But just because the conventional sequence is not psychologically significant, it makes no difference, once we understand the matter rightly, that the sequence *is* thus maintained and never reversed.[1]

In more ways than one, a Greek tragedy was less like a modern stage play than like a modern oratorio or opera; and it may be useful to observe that the lyric-iambic sequence is not unlike the sequence of recitative

[1] The origin of this particular convention, like that of most others, is obscure. As it does not appear in the earlier plays of Aeschylus, we may guess that, whatever its origin, it did not establish itself till towards the middle of the fifth century. If the *Rhesus*, in which it is prominent, is the work of a fourth-century poet, it would seem to have held its ground for a long while. That it is relatively infrequent in the later plays of Euripides is perhaps due to his increasing tendency towards realism. But our statistics are too scanty to allow of any confident conclusion.

and aria regularly found in the 'classical' oratorio and opera of the eighteenth and early nineteenth centuries. In this latter, the order of the sequence is reversed. The recitative corresponds, roughly, to the spoken iambics of Greek tragedy, the aria to the sung lyrics. We need go no further than the oratorios and operas of Handel for abundant illustrations of this conventional form. Here also, the two members of the sequence form an artistic whole, the psychological significance of which would not be altered if the order of the two members were reversed. To the composers of that period, such a reversal would have seemed ridiculous and impossible; and we may assume that the Greek tragic poet would have thought it no less out of the question to reverse the order of the lyric-iambic sequence—not even Euripides ever does this. The more thoroughly a convention becomes established, the more it comes to be regarded not as a mere convention but as the only natural and proper way of doing things. To accept it thus unquestioningly need not hamper, and may help, the writer or composer gifted with creative originality. But if we are to understand the work of such men as the Greek tragic poets, we must distinguish, as clearly as possible, between what is conventional in their work and what is not. To speak generally, what is on the surface is conventional, a complex of set ritual forms, by which, and underlying which, there is suggested to spectator or reader a vivid picture of words and deeds, of feelings and thoughts, no one of which is directly and precisely reproduced either in the text of the play or in its presentation on the stage.

In so far as the conclusions reached in this chapter are sound, there is no need to insist upon their importance for the right understanding of Greek tragedy. It is only because something like them has always been, to some extent, in the minds of scholars and critics, subconsciously active though not explicitly formulated, that this right understanding has in a great measure been achieved. Yet for want of the explicit formulation of them, misunderstandings have befallen the most learned scholars and the most sympathetic and discerning critics; and the errors have not always been trivial. My attempt at such formulation may perhaps sound a note of warning that will do some service to scholars and critics whose learning and acumen are far above my own.

It will not take long to indicate the connexion of the arguments in this final chapter with the rest of the book. So long as the tragedies of Euripides are regarded from an essentially realistic point of view, my main thesis must appear dubious, if not wholly incredible. Despite Voltaire and Shaw and others, the interweaving of religious, moral and political satire with the presentation of a tragic story, and the consequent fictitious or 'fantastic' nature of that story, are ideas which must be instinctively resented as destroying the beauty and significance of Euripides' plays; and the 'bad art' explanation of such facts as cannot be ignored or explained away must be preferred as the less of two evils. This attitude becomes less reasonable as soon as the non-realistic character of all Greek tragedy is recognized. Such recognition does not, of course, in the least tend directly to establish my thesis: if that can be done, it must be done by such arguments as are put forward in the preceding chapters. But it does, or should, prevent such objections to my thesis as are based on canons of criticism derived from modern drama and applicable to modern drama only. Those persons, if there are any such, who are sure that these canons are eternally and universally valid, and are therefore ready to apply them confidently to the drama of all ages and races, cannot be proved wrong—or at least I do not see how to do it. And of course not one of us can, so to speak, get out of his own skin. Our admiration and enjoyment of drama, as of all art, must be mainly spontaneous, determined by the conventions and customs and standards of our own age, and not alterable, in any great measure, by intellectual argument, by discerning, as sheer matter of fact, that other ages did not admire or enjoy drama for the same reasons as our own age, nor expect it to be what our own age expects it to be. There is indeed no theoretical consideration that either can or should prevent our preferring modern drama to ancient, or among the ancients, Sophocles to Euripides, or Aeschylus to either. What is not justified is the view, based on such grounds as I have mentioned, that Euripides cannot possibly have at once been a great artist and done what I have urged that he did. Those grounds, at least, are not good enough either for condemning him as a bad artist or for disproving the conclusions reached in this book. It is possible that he was indeed a bad artist: it is possible that the view of one side of his art maintained in this book is unsound. But the principles by which the former proposition, and even the latter, can rightly be supported must be either such, if such there are, as can be allowed to be universally valid, or else those which, implicitly or explicitly accepted in ancient Greece, were as transitory in their authority as many, perhaps most, of those accepted by ourselves today. Such principles are not easy to come by. But at least we may and should guard against using any others, and refrain from conferring on our personal predilections, or on those of our own age, the dignity of universal laws.

INDEX

142

INDEX

143

INDEX

For EU product safety concerns, contact us at Calle de José Abascal, 56–1°, 28003 Madrid, Spain or eugpsr@cambridge.org.

 www.ingramcontent.com/pod-product-compliance
Ingram Content Group UK Ltd.
Pitfield, Milton Keynes, MK11 3LW, UK
UKHW012332130625
459647UK00009B/240